# TALES
*from the*
# TOWER

# TALES
*from the*
# TOWER

A Personal History of the
James Joyce Tower and Museum
by its Curators

Vivien Igoe and Robert Nicholson

*Edited by Breandán Ó Broin*
*Introduction by Vincent Browne*

MARTELLO

TALES FROM THE TOWER

First published in 2023 by
Martello Publishing
Glenshesk House
10 Richview Office Park
Clonskeagh
Dublin D14 V8C4
Republic of Ireland

www.martellopublishing.ie

Published in association with the Friends of Joyce Tower.
© Martello Publishing, 2023
© Friends of Joyce Tower, 2023

Individual author pieces:
© Vivien Igoe, 2023
© Robert Nicholson, 2023

Photographs copyright of the authors, except where otherwise indicated

The right of Vivien Igoe and Robert Nicholson to be identified as the authors of this work has been asserted in accordance with the provisions of the Copyright and Related Rights Act, 2000.

All rights reserved. No part of this publication may be reproduced in any form or by any means without the prior permission of the publisher.

A CIP catalogue record for this book is available from the British Library.

Print ISBN: 978-1-7396086-2-0
eBook ISBN: 978-1-7396086-3-7

Martello Publishing gratefully acknowledges the financial support of the Friends of Joyce Tower and Dún Laoghaire-Rathdown County Council in the publication of this book.

Printed by L&C Printing Group, Kraków, Poland
Typesetting and design by Niall McCormack
Typeset in 10.5 over 15.5pt Bembo Pro
Cover image *Martello at Sandycove* © Susan Early

10 9 8 7 6 5 4 3 2 1

# CONTENTS

| | |
|---|---|
| About this Book | vi |
| Introduction: How the Friends of Joyce Tower Began<br>*Vincent Browne* | vii |
| Foreword<br>*Julie Larkin* | ix |
| A Brief Chronology of the Joyce Tower<br>*Breandán Ó Broin* | xi |
| The Joyce Tower History 1804–1972<br>*Vivien Veale Igoe* | 1 |
| The Further History 1972–2019<br>*Robert Nicholson* | 69 |
| The Friends of Joyce Tower 2012–22<br>*Séamus Cannon* | 171 |
| A Brief Reading List | 175 |
| Curator Biographies | 177 |
| Acknowledgements | 179 |
| Index | 180 |

# ABOUT THIS BOOK

*Tales from the Tower* is a personal history of the James Joyce Tower and Museum as recalled by its two leading Curators, Vivien Veale Igoe and Robert Nicholson. Both worked in the Sandycove Tower at a time when it was still possible to meet many of the people who knew people who knew Joyce and his contemporaries.

This unique history is published by Martello Publishing, Dublin, in association with the Friends of Joyce Tower, with financial assistance from Friends of Joyce Tower and Dún Laoghaire-Rathdown County Council (DLRCC).

# INTRODUCTION: HOW THE FRIENDS OF JOYCE TOWER BEGAN

*Vincent Browne,*
*founder member, Friends of Joyce Tower*

UNDER ACUTE financial pressure, Fáilte Ireland, the Irish Tourist Board, closed the Tower in 2012. Journalist Vincent Browne stepped into the breach, proposing that the community take action, and not stand idly by:

'About 60 people turned up at the Joyce Tower on a Friday in August 2012 for a hilarious and chaotic meeting; volunteering to staff the Tower once it was to open a few weeks later. Robert Nicholson, the Curator of the Tower, delivered an entertaining presentation of Joyce and his brief sojourn at the Tower – as recorded in the opening paragraphs of *Ulysses*. Rob Goodbody spoke on the history and structure of the Martello Towers. We were ready to rock 'n' roll.

At that meeting we appointed coordinators for each day of the week – Pat Flynn, Kay Gleeson, Sadbh de Barra, Charlie Hulgraine, Tom Fitzgerald, Julia Beckett and Patrick Glynn.

They recruited volunteers from those present. Suzie Barry was to be the overall co-coordinator. The Friends of Joyce Tower came into being.

The origin of the Friends of Joyce Tower was a meeting in the Boulevard café in mid-2012 involving Tom and Mike Fitzgerald, Yvonne Anderson, Anna Scudds, Colin Scudds, myself (Vincent Browne), and one or two others. All were agreed that an effort should be made, with the cooperation of Dún Laoghaire County Council and Bord Fáilte, to have the Joyce Tower kept open on a regular basis with the assistance of volunteers. This to be done without jeopardising the role of any public servant employed in connection with the Tower. It was agreed we would approach Bord Fáilte and Dún Laoghaire County Council, which we did, only to discover there was some bureaucratic hesitancy and an overlap of responsibility for the Tower. We approached the then Minister for Tourism, Leo Varadkar TD, who resolved those impediments. Don McManus of the Dún Laoghaire Business Association was crucial initially in getting the project underway.

Both Bord Fáilte and Dún Laoghaire County Council were supportive from the beginning and helped resolve the initial difficulties. Intrinsic to the venture was that it would be volunteer-led, no bosses.'

# FOREWORD

*Julie Larkin,*
*Chairperson, Friends of Joyce Tower*

THE YEAR 2022 marked the centenary of the publication of *Ulysses*. It was also the sixtieth anniversary of the opening of the Joyce Tower as a museum. On a slightly less momentous note, it was the tenth anniversary of the establishment of the Friends of Joyce Tower (FJT)! This publication brings all three of these anniversaries together in a unique way.

The Joyce Tower is now under the control of Dún Laoghaire-Rathdown County Council, the primary objective of FJT at its foundation. It seemed an appropriate time to capture the experience of previous curators Vivien Igoe and Robert Nicholson, to celebrate their achievements, and to establish a link between their early experience and the new departure. It was a signal way to mark the anniversary year.

The FJT society has accomplished its objective of securing local management of the Tower. It welcomes the establishment of a management board, Joyce Tower and Museum CLG (Company Limited by Guarantee) and the appointment of our new manager/curator, Dr Alice Ryan, a successor to our authors of *Tales from the Tower*.

As often happens, the original FJT initiative resulted in some unexpected but very welcome outcomes. During our ten-year campaign, a new community of Joyceans has been created locally, which has done much to deepen appreciation of Joyce's work. Reading groups, study courses, art exhibitions, concerts, quizzes and trips abroad have enriched the lives of many and sustained us through the years of Covid.

Having accomplished its objective, the Friends of Joyce Tower has decided to dissolve, to avoid confusion at a time of transition. All assets are being transferred to Joyce Tower and Museum CLG (JTM) and will be used to fund specific projects, *Tales from the Tower* being the first. The volunteers will continue to staff the tower under the management of JTM. The contribution made to the visitor experience by volunteers is much commented upon and is a unique feature of a visit to the Tower. It is also a role the volunteers relish.

The publication of *Tales from the Tower* is a fitting way to mark three anniversaries – the centenary of the publication of *Ulysses*, the sixtieth of the museum's opening and the tenth of FJT – as we embark on a new phase in the Tower's history.

# A BRIEF CHRONOLOGY OF THE JOYCE TOWER

*Breandán Ó Broin,*
*Joyce Tower and Museum volunteer*

1804     The eleventh Martello Tower in Ireland is constructed in Sandycove, Co. Dublin as part of a defence system against an anticipated invasion by Napoleon's French Fleet.

1904     James Joyce stays in the Tower for six nights in September, along with Oliver St John Gogarty and Richard Samuel Chenevix Trench.

1922     *Ulysses* is published in Paris by Sylvia Beach, under the imprint of her Parisian bookshop Shakespeare and Company. The novel becomes a literary sensation; its opening episode is set in the Tower.

1937     Michael Scott, an eminent architect, purchases land adjacent to the Tower, designing his family home, 'Geragh'.

1954    Scott purchases the Tower and begins to make plans for turning it into a Joycean Centre. The first 'Bloomsday Pilgrimage' takes place on the day featured in *Ulysses*, 16 June.

1960    Film Director John Huston makes a substantial donation to help restore the Tower, enabling its opening as a museum.

1962    American-born Sylvia Beach, the original publisher of *Ulysses*, visits Sandycove to open the James Joyce Tower and Museum.

1965    Vivien Veale is appointed curator of the James Joyce Museum to begin the process of cataloguing and enriching the collection of Joycean literature and memorabilia.

1972    The Tower reopens following renovations under the patronage of Thomas Keating.

1972–7  Nora Goodbody, Denis Bates and Roland McHugh serve terms as interim curators.

1978    Robert Nicholson becomes curator, overseeing the Tower's continued development as a global literary centre dedicated to the promotion and understanding of Joyce and his works.

*A Personal History of the Joyce Tower and Museum*

2012      The Tower closes to the public, primarily due to State funding cutbacks following a period of national austerity. The closure causes dismay around the literary world.

2012      The Friends of Joyce Tower come together, staffing the Tower with volunteers and opening seven days a week, Christmas Day included.

2014      Admission to the Tower is free, which leads to numbers soaring to unprecedented levels of more than 40,000 visitors each year.

2020      The Covid pandemic leads to another set of temporary closures of the Tower.

2022      The Office of Public Works (OPW) leases the Tower to Dún Laoghaire-Rathdown County Council (DLRCC), replacing Fáilte Ireland. Subsequently, a new management company, Joyce Tower and Museum CLG (JTM), signs a licence with DLRCC to manage the Tower on an ongoing basis.

             Dr Alice Ryan becomes the Tower's first manager/curator of the new JTM management era, charged with guiding the Tower into the future as an academic centre and visitor attraction.

*Authors and curators Robert Nicholson and Vivien Veale Igoe at the Tower in 2022.*

# THE JOYCE TOWER
# HISTORY 1804–1972

*Vivien Veale Igoe,*
curator

'Rather bleak in wintertime, I should say.
Martello you call it?' *(Ulysses.1.541)*\*

~ 1804 ~

In 1804, the Martello Tower at Sandycove was built, modelled on a tower at Cape Mortella, Corsica, which gives the Tower its name.

Constructed as a defence against a possible Napoleonic invasion and sanctioned by the National Defence Act of 1804, the Martello Tower at Sandycove, Co. Dublin is number eleven of sixteen towers, erected between Dublin and Bray. Seventy-four towers were built in Ireland.

The Sandycove Martello Tower is situated overlooking the Forty Foot Bathing Place and the 'snotgreen sea'. Napoleon never showed up in Dublin Bay and the Tower and its garrison survived in relative peace and quiet.

---

\* Citations from *Ulysses* are according to the critically edited reading text, © Hans Walter Gabler, 1984.

## ~ 1904 ~

In 1904, Oliver St John Gogarty rented the Martello Tower in Sandycove for £8 per annum from the British War Department.

It was an arrangement that lasted until 1910, when he subsequently bought it. He used it as a retreat and occasionally had guests, such as Arthur Griffith, who visited the Tower regularly on Sundays, and would sometimes stay for the weekend, when Gogarty was in residence.

From 9 to 14 September, a young James Joyce stayed in the Tower for a visit that would last six nights. Joyce shared it with Gogarty and Richard Samuel Chenevix Trench, an Oxford Anglo-Irish friend of Gogarty's, who had passionately embraced the Irish Literary Revival. Trench was a son of a major general in the British Army, and a grandson of Richard Chenevix Trench, Archbishop of Dublin.

On Sunday, 12 September 1904, William Bulfin, while gathering material for his *Rambles in Eirinn*, fortuitously called to the Tower and recorded the visit in his book, which is the only detached account of life in the Tower during this significant week. Hearing that some men were 'creating a sensation in the neighbourhood', Bulfin and his companion, who were in the area, called 'and were soon climbing a steep ladder which led to the door of the tower. We entered, and found some men of Ireland in possession, with whom we tarried until far on in the morning.' Bulfin, however, found Joyce silent in the lively company of the others; perhaps a foreboding of the gathering tension between Joyce and Trench. Trench's eccentric behaviour would soon prove to be responsible for Joyce's sudden departure from the Tower.

On the following Tuesday night, 14 September, Trench had a nightmare involving a black panther, and screamed. He fired his revolver into the fireplace. Joyce was understandably frightened. Gogarty disarmed Trench. When Trench's fears returned, Gogarty said, 'Leave him to me,' and shot at the pans on the shelf above Joyce's bed, which tumbled down on Joyce. Without a word, Joyce dressed and left for the long walk back to Dublin.

## ~ 1925–54 ~

In 1925 Gogarty sold the Tower to Mrs Catherine Cameron, who lived in the adjoining house, 'Rockfort'.

Subsequently, the Tower then passed on to Michael Scott, an eminent architect. He bought a site from Cameron situated between the Tower and the Forty Foot Bathing Place. In 1937 Scott designed, built and lived in the house on the site he named 'Geragh'. It stands to this day as a fine example of Modernist marine architecture. In 1954, the year of the fiftieth anniversary of Bloomsday, Scott purchased the Tower with the idea of opening it as a museum and monument to Joyce.

With Scott's idea in mind, the Dublin Joyce Society was founded to raise funds, acquire memorabilia, and open the Tower as a museum. The Society comprised a group of early Dublin Joyceans which included Brian O'Nolan (Myles na gCopaleen); Niall Montgomery, a close friend of Samuel Beckett; Seamus Kelly, the journalist, who wrote under the name of 'Quidnunc' for *The Irish Times*; John Garvin, a distinguished civil servant and author; Lennox Robinson, the playwright and producer; and Constantine P. Curran, who first met Joyce in 1899, when they were both students at University College Dublin.

On 16 June 1954, the fiftieth anniversary of the events in *Ulysses*, the Tower became the starting point for a legendary pilgrimage led by poet Patrick Kavanagh and Brian O'Nolan. John Ryan, Anthony Cronin, A. J. Leventhal and Tom Joyce accompanied them in two horse-drawn cabs they hired out for the journey 'at a time when it was neither popular nor profitable' to quote Myles. Similar to 16 June 1904, the original Bloomsday, the weather on the day of the inaugural Bloomsday Pilgrimage was 'mainly cloudy, but with sunny intervals'.

In Kavanagh's words:

> I made the pilgrimage
> In the Bloomsday swelter
> From the Martello Tower
> To the cabby's shelter.
>
> ('Who Killed James Joyce?')

The cabs made their way to the city via Sandymount strand, halting at various pubs along the way where it seemed they were the object of some jibing and jeering: 'Musta forgot the hearse.' John Ryan made a film of the journey, and the event was reported in the press. *The Irish Times* reported: 'Only time will prove whether or not *Ulysses* is one of the world's greatest novels. When the hundredth anniversary of Bloomsday comes around, Leopold Bloom either may be forgotten, or may stand in stony effigy as high as Nelson Pillar now stands today.' Following the publicity of the fiftieth anniversary, some derogatory letters to the editor of *The Irish Times* appeared such as this one from 25 June 1954: 'Now that it has been decided who lived in No. 7 Eccles Street fifty years ago, is it not time that Swift, Wilde and Joyce, were allowed to rest in peace? The ordinary, healthy, and intelligent Dubliner has heard it all, and more than he cares to hear about them ... were it not for American thesis-writers and such like probing literati, Dublin would already have forgotten Joyce and certainly the other two as well. "Bloomsday" means nothing to the generality of citizens – signed D.P.M.'

According to Seamus Kelly, after the 1954 event, the Dublin Joyce Society went into limbo, where it remained until January 1960.

## ~ 1960–64 ~

In January 1960 the film director John Huston revived Michael Scott's plan that the Martello Tower should be turned into a Joyce museum.

Huston, an admirer of Joyce, and later the director of his remarkable last film, *The Dead*, based on Joyce's short story, gave a very generous donation which helped finance the project and got things underway. Discussions ensued between Seamus Kelly and Michael Scott, resulting in most of the original Dublin Joyce Society members reassembling, plus a few new ones. A committee was formed, comprising Padraic Colum, president of the Society, Donagh MacDonagh, chairman, and Sam Suttle, honorary treasurer. John Ryan and Dorothy Cole were honorary secretaries. Committee members included Michael Scott,

John Huston, Denis Johnston, Seamus Kelly, A. J. Leventhal, Niall Montgomery, Niall Sheridan, Seán O'Faoláin and Ernie Anderson. Overseas members included Sylvia Beach, T. S. Eliot, Maria Jolas, Richard Kain, Frances Steloff and Thornton Wilder. Appeals were sent out for funds to have the Tower rehabilitated. Over time, books and Joyce memorabilia were given or loaned.

During 1962, frequent meetings were held in hurried preparation for the opening of the Tower, at the office of Niall Montgomery, 19 Merrion Square, and at The Bailey, 2–3 Duke Street, owned by John Ryan. It was agreed that Sylvia Beach would be the obvious choice to perform the official opening, being the first publisher of *Ulysses* in 1922. It was released under the imprint of her bookshop, Shakespeare and Company, in Paris. Beach had visited the Tower previously in 1960 before visiting the Aran Islands. After climbing the internal narrow spiral stairway, to reach the parapet, Seamus Kelly heard her remark 'When you think of those fellows climbing that, and so drunk most of the time, I don't know how they did it.' Reminiscing on the parapet, she spoke to Kelly about Joyce and said, 'Sometimes some little professor would write about him, and he [Joyce] would be angry at all the mistakes ... but he liked [Stuart] Gilbert and [Herbert] Gorman ... he hated asking favours, and he never kowtowed.'

On 16 June 1962 the sun shone as Sylvia Beach officially opened the Martello Tower as a Joyce museum. It was the fifty-eighth anniversary of Bloomsday. Only a small number of people were invited to attend because of limited space, but when word got round many more turned up. At 3 p.m., on the parapet of the Tower, assisted by John Ryan, Sylvia Beach hoisted the Milesian flag, 'the oldest flag afloat, the flag of the province of Desmond and Thomond, three crowns on a blue field, the three sons of Milesius' (*Ulysses* 12.1308–10).

Donagh MacDonagh organised a *Ulysses* map of Dublin in conjunction with the opening, and composed a poem for Sylvia Beach. Oliver D. Gogarty – son of Oliver St John Gogarty, who appears as Buck Mulligan in *Ulysses* – emerged clutching a copy of the original lease to remind guests that his father, and not Joyce, had paid the rent for the Tower. Sylvia Beach, in an interview with a young newspaper reporter, said that she was the one who created the name of 'Bloomsday' and 'all these American professors use it and it is the only thing I ever thought of and then they don't attribute it to me'. The reporter asked her what she thought of the museum, and she replied, 'I think it is very interesting, very.' He then asked her if she thought Joyce would approve of it. She replied, 'He couldn't help but approve of it.'

A reception followed, which over a hundred guests attended. Michael Scott had erected a marquee in his garden beside the Tower, offering wine, beer and spirits. Among the guests were May Monaghan and Eileen Schaurek, sisters of James Joyce; Maria Jolas, the widow of Eugene Jolas, Joyce's friend in Paris; and Frances Steloff, from the Gotham Book Mart and chairman of the James Joyce Society of New York, the oldest Joyce society in the world, founded in 1947. Also enjoying the occasion, together with many writers, journalists, and overseas scholars, were Dublin Joyceans John Garvin, Denis Johnston, Mary Lavin, Louis MacNeice, Seán O'Faoláin, W. R. Rodgers and David

Norris, then an eighteen-year-old student. In the evening, at the Eblana Theatre under Busárus, there was a performance of *Bloomsday*, an adaptation of *Ulysses* by Alan McClelland, of Envoy and Gemini Productions.

A Joyce Week was held in Dublin from 16 to 23 June 1962 to coincide with the opening of the Sandycove Tower. This was the first-ever series of lectures devoted to Joyce held in Dublin. Dr Eileen MacCarvill of University College Dublin gave the opening lecture on 17 June, followed by a recital of Joyce's songs by Tomás O'Sullivan at the Building Centre, Baggot Street. Other speakers on the following days included Professor Richard Kain from Louisville, Kentucky, Padraic Colum, James Liddy, John Garvin, Dr A.J. Leventhal and Niall Montgomery. Cyril Cusack gave a reading from *Finnegans Wake*.

From 1962, the Dublin Joyce Society, now renamed the Joyce Tower Society, became responsible for the Tower. It was open for the months of June, July, August and September (including Saturdays and Sundays) between 3 and 6 p.m. The remainder of the year, it opened on Saturdays and Sundays only. In 1962 Mrs Dolly Robinson, widow of the playwright Lennox Robinson, acted as curator of the Tower, and remarked, 'if only they would provide me with a mattress and a bell, I could become a very effective concierge'. She was paid a salary of £5 per week, with a view to an increase in a few months if funds were available. Niall MacDonagh, who had just completed six years at Clongowes Wood College, assisted her. During the year, Dolly Robinson suffered from ill health. Niall took over the job, and dealt ably with some unusual requests. An American visitor asked him if he had any James Joyce-embossed toilet paper. The teenager quipped back that he did not have any but he did have some James Joyce wrapping tissue that had been kindly sent by the Gotham Book Mart in New York. He cut off an appropriately sized piece, which he passed to the grateful American, who duly gave him a handsome donation. During the years that followed, the Joyce Tower Society operated the Tower; it had some gifted volunteers, such as the Limerick-born poet Michael Hartnett, who worked on a version of *Tao Te Ching* while employed at the Tower, and the actors Eamon Morrissey and Máire Hastings.

In his poem 'Ulysses', Paul Durcan recalls visiting the Tower aged eighteen on 17 June 1963, and meeting Hartnett. Durcan asked his father for twenty-one shillings to buy a copy of *Ulysses*, and after a disagreement with him about the 'outrageous sum of money' and the 'notoriously immoral book', Durcan took the 46A bus out to the Tower. Relenting, his father followed him and bought a copy of the Bodley Head edition of *Ulysses*. It is interesting to note that the Tower was one of the few places in Ireland where *Ulysses* was on sale in 1963.

During the early 1960s, the Joyce Tower Society ran into financial difficulties: it received no State funding whatsoever. Fortunately, eight regional tourism organisations (later renamed tourism authorities) were established. Ireland East, known as the Eastern Regional Tourism Organisation (Fáilte an Oirthir Teoranta) which was based in Moran Park, Dún Laoghaire, had responsibility for tourism development in counties Dublin, Kildare, Louth, Meath and Wicklow. The first regional tourism manager was Harold Naylor, a Longford man, and a former journalist with *The Irish Times*, who subsequently became chief executive for the Wales Tourist Board. By 1964, with the help of a Bord Fáilte grant, the sale of the Tower and its contents to the Eastern Regional Tourism Organisation was completed and the company assumed responsibility for its operation and development. Some urgent repairs and improvements to the security of the Tower were carried out and it soon reopened to visitors on seven days a week, from July to mid-October.

~ 1965 ~

Under the Tower's new ownership, I was appointed as the first curator.

I had completed a BA degree at University College Dublin in 1964, followed by the Diploma in Librarianship in 1965. My connection with the Joyce Tower had started when I applied for a position as an 'Antiquities Officer' with the Eastern Regional Tourism Organisation, advertised in *The Irish Times* on 5 March 1965. I had studied archaeology as a subject for my degree, and had excavated at the passage grave at Knowth in the Boyne Valley, and worked on the Viking excavation in High Street, Dublin. At the interview on 21 April, Harold Naylor asked me if 'I would prefer to have a stab at Joyce', with the Sandycove Martello Tower in mind, and enquired if I knew anything about James Joyce. I said I had a good knowledge of Joyce and Dublin, and he asked me to submit a treatise, which I did. Coincidentally, Eileen Veale, my mother, was an avid reader and had read all Joyce's works, including *Finnegans Wake*! She had brought me to all the Dublin locations connected with Joyce when I was a child.

## *A Personal History of the Joyce Tower and Museum*

On Midsummer Day 1965, I started work in the Martello Tower. I lived in Churchtown, and caught two buses to get to Sandycove; it took well over an hour and a half to reach my destination. There were occasional bus strikes, which proved tiresome, and occasionally, when I couldn't get a lift, I cycled the long and hilly journey on my bike. Later on, the tourism organisation had a Honda motorcycle, which I hired for thirty shillings a week. It was very convenient because I now did the journey in half an hour, taking a short cut up through Mount Merrion and down Mount Merrion Avenue to the coast road. In the winter, it could be desperately cold and sometimes icy, but it was still preferable to taking a bus.

Sandycove was heavenly in those days. There was little traffic and seldom any cars parked by the roadside. On the pathway leading up to the Tower, I encountered 'the lobster man' on his bike, going to check his lobster pots. He also had lobster pots in Bulloch Harbour. There was a friendly lady named Mrs. O'Brien who looked after a huge flowerbed at the corner of Otranto Place and Sandycove Avenue West. She had flowers for all seasons, and was always out tending to the common patch of ground. There was a large square wooden sign at the entrance to the Forty Foot Bathing Place indicating that it was reserved for men only. There was another sign on the wall which read, 'Dogs & Bicycles prohibited from entering Forty Foot.' I met the regular hardy swimmers, some of them quite elderly, heading for their dip early each morning, even in the depths of winter. A wall, just over six feet in height, enclosed the area around the Tower, with a small entrance gate at the front, which was kept locked. Inside the gate, the ground was covered with gravel. When I climbed up the iron stairway, which was fifteen feet above the ground, and opened the ponderous black door, I entered 'the gloomy domed livingroom of the tower' (as described in 'Telemachus'), and my desk was situated on the right-hand side, the less draughty side.

The exhibition space was confined solely to this circular room, formerly the Tower's living quarters. The room contained a fireplace, and was lit by two slanted apertures, which Joyce called 'barbicans'. There were five display cases containing artefacts placed at intervals around the wall, two on one side of the fireplace, and three on the other. There were three upright glass frames against the wall, and a glass bookcase, which contained some books. That made up the entire exhibition space of the museum, which at the time was adequate. I bought yards of black velvet and lined each display case. One of the cases contained the original key to the Tower. It was made of copper so that it wouldn't give off sparks and ignite dynamite formerly stored in the gunpowder magazine, now used as a storage room, in the area below.

A large portrait of James Joyce by Basil Blackshaw was placed above the fireplace. There were some framed paintings on the wall, among them a portrait of Joyce by Seán O'Sullivan, RHA, Paris, 1937, loaned by Seamus Kelly. Joyce's death mask, which was bronze and coloured green, was affixed to the wall. This was a pull or copy made from the original death mask, created by the sculptor Paul Speck. Carola Giedion-Welcker in Zurich entrusted an original one to Michael Scott for the Joyce Museum, which was removed, but is now reinstalled. John Joyce's waistcoat,

## A Personal History of the Joyce Tower and Museum

sometimes worn by his son James, was of interest, having been donated by Samuel Beckett.

The narrow winding interior stone staircase, contained within the wall, led to the top of the Tower, enclosed by a stone deck, with a raised portion, or gun rest, in the centre. The staircase also led down to the area below, now divided into two empty rooms, which had originally been a single-space location of the gunpowder magazine. Despite the walls being eight feet thick, it was continually cold, draughty and damp because the granite walls had a tendency to weep non-stop. There was a 'storage heater', which emitted scant heat. There was also a blow-heater if it got really cold, but it never really heated the place adequately. Initially, there was no telephone, which was scary, because there were rumours around about a peculiar character wandering in the vicinity. However, the concerned Gardaí from both Dalkey and Dún Laoghaire stations called when they were in the area to check on me, and brought me chocolate.

No typewriter was supplied, so I brought my own portable Olivetti, along with plenty of carbon paper, to keep copies of reports and correspondence. If I made a typing error, there was no such thing as correcting fluid – only a pencil-shaped rubber eraser, which was difficult to manoeuvre, and could tear the paper if used! I had a small cash box; the entrance charge was a shilling. I sold black-and-white postcards and paperback books on Joyce, so there was some bookkeeping to be done each week. I left my post and the cash down to the head office in Moran Park at lunchtime. Occasionally, as a treat, I stopped at Dún Laoghaire Baths, and had a 'hot sea bath' which cost three shillings and sixpence. There were little rooms, each containing a huge big bath. There was loads of piping hot sea water gushing out of big brass taps. It was almost possible to float on top of the water, the bath was so large. It was a great amenity and it is a tragedy that the baths and swimming pools closed forever. Sometimes, it proved difficult to find someone to work weekends, as staff members didn't like the idea of working in the Tower, with its lack of facilities. So occasionally I worked seven days a week. Later on, I was fortunate that a totally reliable, charming and well-read local woman, Nora Goodbody, worked at the weekends. She lived nearby and cycled down, propping her unlocked bike by the Tower. In those days, there was no need to lock your bike!

Apart from the regional head office, some of the staff worked in the local tourist office, located on the ground floor in the same building as the former Fuller's coffee shop (now demolished) on Marine Road, while others serviced the offices in the five counties in the region. The tourism network was efficiently organised, as staff were brought on familiarisation trips, and were well versed on the various tourist attractions in each county. In this way, interested tourists were directed to the Tower. We also had a smart uniform, which was revised every couple of years to a new design. I had three different uniforms in five years! As in Joyce's time, there was no plumbing in the Tower, and consequently no toilet or running water, except the water running down the walls. It remained like that for the duration of my duties there. Plumbing wasn't installed until years later.

Sometimes I brought a flask, as there were no cafés close at hand, though there was a nice bakery shop in Glasthule where

## A Personal History of the Joyce Tower and Museum

I bought cream buns. Sometimes I joined my colleagues and friends, Áine McManus, Tom Murphy and Michael Burke from headquarters at Moran Park, and we had soup and a sandwich at Mooney's pub in Upper George's Street, Dún Laoghaire, while catching up with the local tourism news and other gossip.

The wooden floor in the Tower tended to get dusty, and was washed periodically with buckets of sea water, hauled up the iron staircase. At the outset there was no cleaner, so I had to organise the cleaning myself. Annie, a cleaning woman from Glasthule who cleaned the head office in Moran Park, appeared occasionally. In one way, she was more of a hindrance than a help, in so far as she never actually stuck to just cleaning the place. When a coach load of tourists entered, she would liven up considerably and stop work. Pausing for the last of the group to arrive, she would then lean on the handle of her mop, and exclaim in a loud voice 'I have lived in this district for well over sixty-five years and that fellow James Joyce never lived in this tower, so I don't know why you are all coming here.' Nothing that I ever said to her would stop her holding forth before her captive audience.

There was a small library in the Tower which contained a copy of *A Wake Newslitter*, a periodical devoted to *Finnegans Wake*. It gave the names of the editors – Fritz Senn in Zurich, and Professor Clive Hart in Australia – both of whom I contacted. I also contacted Professor Tom Staley at the University of Tulsa, Oklahoma, editor of the *James Joyce Quarterly*, which he had started in 1963, aged twenty-seven, when he was just two years out of graduate school. All replied promptly, friendly links were forged and a worldwide network was created. As Fritz Senn later remarked to me, 'Those years in the 1960s were really productive and we never thought what we were about to unleash.' He never said a truer word! In those early days, the international Joycean community was small, and we all knew one another, or certainly about one another. One of my primary aims when I started at the Tower was to build up a reference library with books, journals, periodicals, pamphlets and newspapers cuttings. I bought books, cajoled books from authors who called, and wrote to publishers all over the world for copies of their Joyce publications. The response from Joycean authors was remarkable, with signed books and articles arriving frequently. From 1962 right up to the present, a visitors' book was kept. Unfortunately, the earlier two most important books dating from the opening of the museum in 1962, which recorded the signatures of Sylvia Beach, Joyce's sisters, Maria Jolas and Frances Steloff, and all those present, were dumped by a senior staff member when in winter storage at head office in Moran Park. This was a tragic loss of important archival material.

The first Irish visitor to the Tower was Gerry O'Flaherty, a Joycean enthusiast of international repute, and an authority on his native city. He knew more about Joyce and his native Dublin than anyone I ever met. From the mid-1950s, he assisted American Joycean researchers such as Richard Ellmann with their lists of queries; he also corresponded with Dr Harley K. Croessmann from 1953 to 1962. The Croessmann Collection of James Joyce is substantial and contains correspondence by and about Joyce, along with many manuscripts, galley proofs, notes, and pictorial representations by Joyce and his friends, biographers and critics.

## A Personal History of the Joyce Tower and Museum

On 8 July 1965 Harry Pollock, the founder of the James Joyce Society in Canada, was another early visitor. Pollock had produced some Joyce works on stage in Canada. He felt an affinity to Leopold Bloom because he also worked in advertising. He invited me to speak at the Joyce Society in Canada, but in those days it would have been out of the question to find the means to travel to Toronto to give a lecture on Joyce. However, it was nice to be invited! The same month, a pleasant, unobtrusive young gentleman from New York named Byrne called. He spent the afternoon in the Tower looking around at the exhibits and talking about his father, John Francis Byrne, who had lived in 7 Eccles Street before he emigrated to the US in February 1910. He said that Joyce was a frequent visitor during the two trips he made to Dublin in 1909 and on occasion stayed overnight in this house with his father, and had later used it as the home of the Blooms in 1904. He added that his father was a close friend of James Joyce and was 'Cranly' in *A Portrait of the Artist as a Young Man* and in *Ulysses*. The father's memoir, *Silent Years*, was published in 1953. Mr. Byrne was a mirror image of J.F. Byrne as depicted in the photograph with George Clancy and James Joyce at UCD (Croessmann Collection). I felt privileged to have met him. He said that if I ever visited New York to be sure to call on him. He left his address, which unfortunately I mislaid.

At the time, 7 Eccles Street was put up for sale. The vendors were not offered enough money for it and withdrew the property. It was later put on the market again and eventually demolished, like many other houses of historic and literary interest in Dublin. Professor Richard Kain, one of the earliest American

Joyce scholars to visit Dublin, called with a staff member from RTÉ. They were preparing to make a film for the twenty-fifth anniversary of Joyce's death in 1966. I never saw the film, but maybe if it was made it is now in some university archive. Kain, who was at the opening of the museum, kindly donated a copy of his book *Dublin in the Age of William Butler Yeats and James Joyce* (1962). His other books include *Fabulous Voyager*, one of the earliest significant critical works on Joyce, which was published in 1947, and *The Man, the Work, the Reputation* (1956).

Michael Scott, a founder of the museum and next-door neighbour, regularly bounded in to say 'hello' and to look at the new books on Joyce which I was constantly adding to the collection.

That summer was the worst for twenty-six years. In mid-September, there was a nasty downpour which penetrated through the ceiling of the Tower and soaked the entire place, including some of the books. All the damage and smell of dampness bothered me. Most of the morning was spent with a bucket and mop. I really have no idea what I would have done without that bucket and mop! Things brightened up considerably with the arrival of a letter from Fritz Senn, and an invitation to Zurich.

A ferocious fog enveloped the Dún Laoghaire area on 6 October, which was Ivy Day. Everyone was coughing! The visibility from the Tower was two yards. When I looked over the parapet all I could see was grey – nothing else. The fog was so ghostly the mail boat couldn't even berth. The ship lay offshore for fourteen hours with supplies being delivered to it. Despite the elements, the first season proved successful, with the total number of visitors to the museum numbering 2,248 between 15 July and

15 October. Not every day was busy; on some days only four people called.

There were very few visitors from Ireland. The attitude the Irish had towards Joyce and his works in those days was one of suspicion and indifference. He was seen as anti-Irish and anti-Catholic. After closing the Tower one day and heading down past the Forty Foot on the way to the bus stop, I encountered a senior academic staff member from UCD. I joyfully told her about my new and exciting job; she stared at me, and said, 'Miss Veale, you should be utterly ashamed of yourself. You are working in a sewage museum.' Most of the visitors were from the United States and Europe and certainly didn't share her attitude. Some American students made the journey solely to see the Tower and Joyce's Dublin. They would cross the threshold, be silent for a minute, and then exclaim: 'I can't believe it. I can't really believe I am here.' Even Americans returning from Vietnam stopped off at Dublin just to visit the Tower.

Other significant arrivals during the first momentous year included Sergio Vilar, a noted journalist from the magazine *Destino* in Barcelona. A feature following his visit appeared in the popular French literary review *Les Lettres Nouvelles, Mars–Avril 1966,* resulting in great publicity for the Tower. V.S. Pritchett, the British writer and literary critic whose family moved frequently like the Joyce family, also called. His memoir, *A Cab at the Door*, was published in 1968.

In mid-October, the 1965 season ended, and the Tower closed for the winter months. I transferred to head office in Moran Park, Dún Laoghaire. I dealt with Joycean correspondence, and spent time in the National Library doing research, and copying out by hand the entire catalogue of the Joyce entries. My intention was to get all the items listed in the catalogue! I bought books for the collection and worked on an index of the antiquities in the five counties of the eastern region. The position of 'Antiquities Officer' which I had originally applied for was never filled; however, that didn't dim my interest in archaeology.

## ~ 1966 ~

In February 1966 I travelled to Zurich to meet Fritz Senn, who later became Director of the Zurich James Joyce Foundation which was established in 1985.

Fritz informed me that he would carry a copy of *Ulysses* under his arm so I would recognise him, and not to expect someone in lederhosen! Arriving at Zurich airport, I encountered Clive Hart, one of the editors of the *A Wake Newslitter*, who had been staying with Fritz, and who was dashing out across the runway to catch a flight to Rome. We just had time to say a quick 'hello'. In those days there was no coach to deliver you to your plane – you walked or ran! Fritz introduced me to Joyce's friend Paul Ruggiero. He had informed Ruggiero about the Joyce Museum in the Martello Tower, and the lack of material in it.

Fritz's generosity knew no bounds. He left no stone unturned during my visit, and brought me to all the Joyce haunts, which included the apartments at Universitätstrasse No. 29, and No. 38 where Joyce started back into work on *Ulysses*. The city authorities had erected a plaque there. We also visited Reinhardstrasse 7, Kreuzstrasse 19, and Seefeldstrasse 54 and 73. It

## A Personal History of the Joyce Tower and Museum

was particularly exciting to visit the Kronenhalle restaurant, which Joyce frequented during 1940 and 1941, and to actually meet and speak with some of the waitresses who remembered him. They remarked that they liked him because he was very friendly. Nora and Joyce's son, Giorgio, also came here after Joyce's death. It was a typical old-style Zurich restaurant and had not changed since Joyce's time. There was an original Picasso hanging on the wall. Painted around the walls were the historical craft guilds of Zurich with their coats of arms.

A highlight of my visit was meeting Paul Ruggiero and his wife Bertha. He was an incredibly generous man, and donated material for the Joyce Tower, for which he had been offered large sums of money. In pride of place among the valuable memorabilia Ruggiero donated was Joyce's guitar, which Joyce had given to him as a present. Before handing it to me, Ruggiero sang a Greek love song that he and Joyce often used to sing together. I felt quite sad as I listened to his clear, beautiful voice, while he played the guitar he loved so much for the last time. He also parted with Joyce's cigar case; a signed copy of *Dubliners*, which Joyce had given him and Bertha as a wedding present; five postcards from Joyce to him dating from 1917-23; three letters from Joyce to him, all written in Italian; and other treasured and valuable items. It was through Fritz Senn and his friendship with Ruggiero that the Tower received such a generous donation, which today forms a unique and valuable part of the museum's collection.

Des Rushe reported on my visit to Switzerland in his 'Tatler' column in the *Irish Independent:* 'Miss Veale is an intelligent and charming young girl who has made close contact with Joyce fans throughout the world. She went to Switzerland in connection with the Tower, and met Fritz Senn, joint publisher of the Joycean *A Wake Newslitter*, and Paul Ruggiero, who was an intimate friend of Joyce in Zurich. Because of her personal qualities, she was presented with several items for display in the Tower, which others could not hope to buy for any money. Included is a guitar with which Joyce often accompanied himself when singing; three rare photographs of the writer, one of which has never been published before; a number of greeting cards written by Joyce; a monetary statement of Joyce's financial position in 1940; a wine list which the writer signed in the Kronenhalle Restaurant Zurich; a unique recording of a reading from *Finnegans Wake* in German; and several more relics. The Sandycove Tower continues to grow in stature as a tourist attraction, and the treasure which she has brought back from Zurich will add considerably to its interest this year.'

On 8 March 1966, very early in the morning, the upper part of the Nelson Pillar in O'Connell Street was seriously damaged by a powerful explosion. After work that day, I dashed in to see it; all that remained of it was a stump, with a huge amount of rubble strewn across the street. I thought of the 'Onehandled adulterer' and the 'Parable of the Plums' in the 'Aeolus' episode in *Ulysses*, when two Dublin women make a special trip to the Nelson Pillar and, having reached the top, spit plum stones down on the people below. I retrieved a piece of the pillar for display in the Tower as the pillar is cited a dozen times in *Ulysses*.

On 16 March there was a meeting in the Tower with Harold Naylor, the Regional Tourism Manager, and Dermot O'Toole,

## A Personal History of the Joyce Tower and Museum

an architect. After a lengthy discussion it was suggested that a copper dome be erected over the top of the parapet. I said that I would rather sit in the Tower with the rain pouring in than have a copper dome! The proposal never materialised.

What was interesting about working at the Tower was the diversity of people who visited. I encountered writers, poets, artists, film directors, translators and people of all creeds and convictions. All the major Joycean academics and translators called, as well as students writing theses on Joyce. You never knew who was going to walk in the door. They all had their own story to tell, and tell it they did. The Tower became a dedicated hub for the dissemination of Joycean information. If anyone wanted to know what was going on, they phoned me. Eileen MacCarvill, a former lecturer of English at UCD, phoned me at least three times a week to find out who had called and what they had said. Eileen Schaurek's daughter, Bozena Delimata, who was Joyce's exotic niece and lived near the Tower, also liked to be kept in the loop. She was a friend of my mother's and they often went on excursions together. Bozena frequently invited me to her house where she kept wolfhounds. It was fascinating to listen to her speaking about her uncle Jim and his daughter, Lucia.

On the opening day for the 1966 season in May, no one called in the morning. In the afternoon, I heard the sound of the heavy step of Patrick Kavanagh climbing the iron staircase. He wasn't very robust, and with each step he muttered the Holy Name. He considered himself a friend of the family, and frequently called to our home in Churchtown. The Tower was familiar territory to Kavanagh, who had been associated with it since 1954. Kavanagh would plonk himself on the wicker chair and while away the time, talking about his home in Inniskeen in County Monaghan, and discussing various topics such as the time of the premiere of the ballet *Gamble No Gamble*, staged in the Abbey Theatre in 1961. He often referred back to this event with a sense of satisfaction. The ballet had connections with his long-time friend John Ryan, whom he had known since 1949, when Ryan founded and edited *Envoy*, a monthly literary magazine to which Kavanagh contributed a diary. Ryan designed the set for *Gamble No Gamble* and Kavanagh wrote the words. Ryan's wife Patricia, director of the National Ballet, was the choreographer, and the role of the gambler was divided between the actor T.P. McKenna, who was the narrator, and Charles Schuller, a dancer from London. Ciara O'Sullivan, who was attached to the Abbey – and was the Rose of Tralee in 1962 – was one of the principal dancers. At the end of the performance, Kavanagh, attired in a dress suit and bow tie, was ushered on to the stage to take a curtain call, from where he addressed the audience at length, taking a lot of credit for the show! I was in the audience, and recall that evening clearly. During the summer of 1966, an art exhibition by Australian artist Val Harford, entitled 'One Blooming Day', was mounted on the walls in the lower area of the Tower. This collection, which consisted of twenty-four Joycean paintings, widened the public interest, and was something extra for the visitor to view. It also made good use of the space.

On 25 May, I had the privilege of meeting the legendary Frances Steloff from the Gotham Book Mart for the first time. Born in Saratoga Springs in New York State in 1887, Frances

*A Personal History of the Joyce Tower and Museum*

came from a poor background, sold flowers as a child, and later became the founder and proprietor of the famous bookshop on West Forty-Seventh Street in New York, from where she pushed Joyce's work into circulation. She called, accompanied by May Joyce Monaghan and my mother, Eileen Veale. After closing time, we went to see 1 Martello Terrace, Bray, the house where May was born in 1890, and where the Christmas dinner scene took place in *A Portrait of the Artist as a Young Man*. The Joyce family had lived there from 1887 to 1891. Frances was ecstatic to see May's birthplace and the promenade along the sea front where the Joyce children played. We visited numerous other places, and returned home well after midnight with the moon shining brightly in the sky. Frances inscribed on a copy of *Wise Men Fish Here; the Story of Frances Steloff and the Gotham Book Mart* by W.G. Rogers (1965). It read:

> For Eileen and Vivien Veale in grateful memory of a happy day and the hope of another soon.
> Love Frances Steloff, May 25th 1966.

On 10 June, Joseph Strick, the film director, and Fred Haines, his assistant, came to discuss the possibility of using the Tower for his film of *Ulysses*. The Company agreed that the Tower would be made available for the film. I met Joseph Strick frequently, as I did research for him on some of the characters in *Ulysses*, mainly Molly Bloom. On the eve of Bloomsday 1966, I organised a small function at which John Garvin, one of Ireland's foremost Joyceans, gave a lecture entitled 'Portrait of the Artist in *Finnegans*

*Wake*'. As well as members of the press, thirty guests attended, including Joseph Strick, Eileen MacCarvill, Seamus Kelly, Eileen Veale, Mervyn Wall, Ulick O'Connor, Gerard O'Flaherty and Noel Carroll, the Olympian and stalwart staff member of the organisation, who later championed the Dublin City Marathon.

Bloomsday 1966, the twenty-fifth anniversary of the year of James Joyce's death, went unmarked in Dublin. But the City Council of Zurich held a 1966 Bloomsday celebration and commemoration of James Joyce at the Great Hall of the University of Zurich. The occasion was the unveiling of a bronze monument by the Rome-based American sculptor Milton Hebald at the writer's grave. I received an invitation on 20 May to the event, but as it was a busy period at work, I was unfortunately unable to attend. Both John Garvin and Donagh MacDonagh attended. Garvin, invited by the Cultural Relations Committee in conjunction with the University of Zurich, gave the lecture he had given in the Joyce Tower the previous evening. Richard Ellmann, Joyce's biographer, also spoke. Bloomsday at the Tower was disappointing because of the lack of interest by the Irish. The majority of visitors who called were from overseas: Finns, Swedes, Americans and even a Greenlander. Professor Roger McHugh from UCD dashed in to pay his respects. Without fail, he always called on Bloomsday. A telegram from Zurich arrived which read: 'Bloomsday Greetings from Fritz Senn, Donagh MacDonagh and Milton Hebald'. On 22 June, Richard Ellmann, accompanied by Professor O'Neill from Ottawa, strolled into the Tower. Ellmann enquired, 'Are you Miss Veale?' I said I was, and we had a long and interesting conversation. He said he would see me in 'the fall'.

## *A Personal History of the Joyce Tower and Museum*

On 10 July, it rained all day. Joseph Strick, accompanied by Graham Probst, the film's artistic director, two prop girls and other helpers arrived at the Tower at 6 p.m. to set up the Tower for the filming of the film *Ulysses*. All the display cases and their contents were removed and stored, and beds and props were moved into the Tower to recreate how it looked in September 1904. The walls were given a fresh coat of paint. We were working through the night into the early hours of the following morning, carrying things up and down the iron staircase non-stop. Between 10 and 13 July, the Tower remained closed to the public for the shooting of *Ulysses*. T.P McKenna played the part of Buck Mulligan; Maurice Roeves, who had a Scottish accent, played Stephen Dedalus; and Graham Lines, who studied philosophy at Oxford, played Haines. The film included not only shots in the Tower, but fine views of Dublin Bay.

On 11 July, just before 7 a.m. on what was a beautiful, bright day, the film crew arrived in a bus filled with cameramen, sound technicians, and the director's assistants. The make-up and wardrobe staff had arrived earlier. A canteen followed, pulled by a jeep. This was parked in the space at the entrance to the Forty Foot Bathing Place. The Tower was packed with equipment, wires, lighting and people. The scene on the parapet was filmed in the morning, with shaving cream blowing all over the place.

Later, I went to Ardmore Studios in Bray with Graham Probst to see the rushes of the film. It was impressive to see the results of the previous day's filming on the screen. On 14 July, filming continued at the Forty Foot, where T.P. McKenna proved to be a great attraction. The Tower was left in disarray after the filming, and the showcases were not reinstalled until a few days afterwards, so it still retained the 1904 appearance. During that period, a few visitors who called and saw the bed in the Tower, enquired, 'Do you live here?'

When *Ulysses* the film was finally released, a letter appeared in one of the newspapers, which read: 'Your correspondent Mr Seamus O'Mairtin goes into a tizzy about the film *Ulysses* and says it has "beauty, poetry and honesty". On the contrary, it is cheap, vulgar and pornographic. Even the hardened film critics at the Cannes Film Festival described it as filthy and obscene. D.F. Conlan.'

It was obvious that the public's attitude to Joyce had really not changed much. After the release of Joseph Strick's film *Ulysses* in 1967, a letter appeared in an Irish paper from a reader who had seen the film in London:

> As an Irishman, having just seen *Ulysses* in London, I must tell you that this film is bad publicity for our country. The film itself was quite a new experience, as never before have we heard sex discussed so freely on the screen. It is likely to give foreigners the impression that the Irish people are Godless, and Dublin a city full of prostitutes and brothels. A certain amount of this may be true, but it is not publicised which is a good thing. Now, however, it should be considered likely that this film may cause tourists to think that Dublin is another city full of 'La Dolce Vita', the consequences of which would be unfortunate. I feel that a team of Irish journalists should come over here to London to see it and then inform the Irish people of the

facts about it. One wonders why Irish actors took part in this film; not to mention the possibility that they may be Roman Catholic too.

There was another bus strike in August. One day, I cycled from Churchtown to Dún Laoghaire in the pelting rain, which took three-quarters of an hour, going mostly downhill. By the time I reached Head Office in Moran Park, I was drenched. I continued to the Tower in gale-force winds with high waves dashing against the rocks in Scotsman's Bay, just in case there were any visitors, but no one turned up. I should have realised that no one would be foolish enough to venture out. By the time I arrived home that evening, I was soaked again. The following day the weather had improved, but the buses were still on strike. So yet again I cycled to the Tower. During the morning, when I was affixing two pages together, a staple went through one of my fingers. It was excruciatingly sore, but a visitor removed it with pliers, which, luckily, he happened to have in his pocket. There was never a first-aid box kept on the premises. There was no such thing as Health and Safety in those days!

August 1966 was a busy time. The summer months rolled on, and in early August a visitor from Connecticut called and, after spending the afternoon at the Tower, offered me a job teaching at a school. I was often offered jobs, but I was interested in what I was doing, so I stayed put. Maurice Roeves, who had played the part of Stephen Dedalus in the film of *Ulysses*, arrived one morning to the Tower shivering and soaking wet. He said he had fallen into the sea. I wasn't much help because I had no towels to dry him! He eventually retreated. A few days later, Professor Virginia Moseley, from the University of Texas, called. I was expecting her. She had hired a little red Mini car. She handed me the key and I drove her around all the Joycean places in Dublin, from Bray to Chapelizod. She wrote *Joyce and the Bible* (1967) and remained a friend for many years. The flag, which Sylvia Beach had launched at the Tower at the official opening in 1962, was now in tatters. So I replaced it, and gave the original to Clive Hart. It was later returned to the archive at Museum of Literature Ireland (MoLI), in Newman House, St Stephen's Green.

It was lunchtime, and I was sitting down by the rocks dangling my feet in the water, eating sandwiches with my friend Áine McManus from Moran Park, when David Ward, from Tulsa, Oklahoma appeared for the first time. Tall, lanky and wearing cowboy boots, he was leaning against the wall waiting for the Tower to open. David was assistant editor of the recently established *James Joyce Quarterly*, and was one of the early core-group members of the international Joyceans. He later played a major role in Joyce affairs, helping with the legal framework to set up the James Joyce Foundation.

Some days later, Clive Hart was in the Tower, when Mr Fitzpatrick from Fitzpatrick Travel Films, Hollywood, California, arrived with his cameraman. He was a guest of the Tourist Board and was making a travel film about places of literary interest in Ireland. He said that when he had finished the film and it went on release, it would bring thousands of visitors to Ireland, as it would be shown to over 59 million people in five languages. Clive and I featured in the film talking about the few days Joyce spent in the

## A Personal History of the Joyce Tower and Museum

Tower with Gogarty and Trench in September 1904. We never saw the film and were not launched to stardom as a result of our appearance!

The Italian National Television production team arrived soon after to make a film. In addition, radio broadcasters frequently called to interview me, asking all sorts of questions about Joyce, the Tower, and the people who called. One went so far as to ask me had James Bond ever called, to which I replied 'not recently'. Belgium radio called and then repaired to The Bailey pub in Duke Street, and recorded on tape the sound of someone knocking with their fist on the door of 7 Eccles Street because the knocker was missing. The door was kept at the time in The Bailey before moving to the Joyce Centre, North Great George's Street.

*Tales from the Tower* would be incomplete without a seafaring story. The rocks to the east of Dalkey Island are known as the Muglins and are mentioned in *Ulysses*. They are visible from the Tower but you can't see Dalkey Island from there. One sunny morning, Clive Hart sauntered in and suggested we take a trip to Dalkey Island on my lunchtime break to check on the Muglins. As a strict timekeeper and never late for work, I didn't think there would be sufficient time for such a trip, but Clive assured me he was a competent man with an oar. Hiring a rowing boat at Coliemore Harbour, we made the journey in both directions in record time, but on the way back, Clive insisted we stop for lunch at the Coliemore Hotel which overlooked the harbour. He had a couple of glasses of Nuits-Saint-Georges to accompany his meal. Arriving back to the Tower a little late, I handed the key to Clive, as I couldn't face the wrath of the visitors who had been kept waiting outside. He gladly accepted it and acted as curator for the afternoon, a task he thoroughly enjoyed!

That summer, I had an unusual visitor: a racing pigeon. He stopped, overcome with exhaustion, and remained in a nook off the parapet. He made no effort to take flight, so I did my research on ailing pigeons, bought special pigeon food and provided water for my feathered friend. After a fortnight, he succumbed. He had a ring on his leg giving his identification, and I discovered that he was from a club in Wales which I contacted. I wrote and told them the fate of the pigeon, and that I had buried him at sea. I received a really nice letter of thanks from his owner, who said he would come over to the Tower and thank me personally.

Fredric Seiden, a young American student who was on a visit to Dublin from 6 to 12 July 1966, rented a bike, and cycled to the Tower from the city. When he paid his shilling at the entrance, he enthusiastically related to me that he had visited 7 Eccles Street the previous day, and had removed the knocker from the door, seeing that the adjoining houses were due to be demolished. He then proudly plonked the knocker on my desk for me to examine. I presumed that he would leave it with me for the museum and encouraged him to do so, but he said he was taking it to show the folks back home and would return it someday. True to his word, Seiden returned to Dublin with the knocker, and officially handed it back at a special ceremony and celebration at the James Joyce Centre, North Great George's Street, on 12 June 2013, forty-seven years later! As Seiden remarked, it was a bit like *Finnegans Wake*, which goes around in a circle. It was a memorable day for both of us to meet up again, and for the knocker to be replaced on the door of 7 Eccles Street!

Other visitors in 1966 included Mikael Urnov, the chief of the Foreign Writers' Union in Moscow, who was a keen and interested visitor. He knew every corner of Dublin and wrote articles on Joyce in *Kunst und Literatur*; James Atherton, one of the foremost Joyce scholars at this time and author of *The Books at the Wake: A Study of Literary Allusions in James Joyce's Finnegans Wake* (1959); Cyril Pearl, a prominent Australian journalist who was researching for his book *Dublin in Bloomtime: The City James Joyce Knew*, published in 1969; and Clem Semmler, the Australian author, broadcaster and literary critic, also met with a warm welcome.

This was the summer that Roland McHugh made his first appearance, when one day he wandered in resembling a fresh-faced schoolboy. He spoke enthusiastically about the research work he was doing on entomology (the study of insects) and on Joyce. Roland was later to work as Curator of the Tower for two seasons. Author of a number of books, his classic reference work, *Annotations to Finnegans Wake*, was first published in 1980. Another notable visitor was Marjorie Barkentin, who adapted and dramatised *Ulysses in Nighttown* from Joyce, with some good advice from Padraic Colum. *The New York Times* had this to say about the play: 'This play gives a vivid picture of the dark seamy labyrinth of the mind of a worldly but unsophisticated man, gross, vain, sentimental, hypocritical, naïve, doomed.'

Professor Eitaro Murayama from Japan, who was working on a translation of *Ulysses*, also called. He was in Dublin to locate all the places mentioned in *Ulysses*. I took him on a detailed tour, and you never saw a happier man. He had written to me on previous occasions, asking questions like, 'The Sun Dial on James's Street. I want to know the shape of this monument, its coming into existence.' So, I went to James's Street and sketched it for him. He also asked about Benson's Ferry, Ringabella and Ringaskiddy (in County Cork), the Smoothing-Iron, and names from fascinating old Dublin. I learned a lot myself, by finding out detailed information for others. I received many queries from all over the world.

Alexander Louis Theroux, an unusual student from the University of Charlottesville in Virginia, called with his friend Julie. He had long, thick black hair, which was blowing in an unruly fashion in all directions. He told me he had been in a Franciscan seminary in New York for two years; then in a Trappist monastery in Massachusetts for two and a half years. He quit the monastic life and was studying English literature. When he saw Joyce's waistcoat on display, he wanted a photograph taken of him wearing it! I politely informed him that it was too small to fit him, that Joyce was slimmer than he was. He said he would like to meet Joyce's sister May Monaghan, and could I arrange a meeting? I phoned May to see if she was agreeable, and she invited me to come to her house in Terenure and to bring Alex and Julie along. So, we had tea with May; then May, Eileen Veale, Alex, Julie and I went to the Abbey Tavern in Howth that evening to hear ballad singing, which was very popular in the 1960s. When the ballad singers heard that May was in the audience, they sang *Finnegans Wake*. Theroux is a novelist and poet in the US.

## *A Personal History of the Joyce Tower and Museum*

Visitors from Sweden included Professor Johannes Hedberg from Gothenburg University, who said that rather late in life he fell for Ireland and the Irish and, more especially, for James Joyce. Magnus Hedlund, a writer of many articles both on Joyce and Beckett and some highly acclaimed novels, wandered in one morning. He was a quiet, thoughtful young man, with a handsome Viking face. He was wearing wooden clogs, which made an unusual echo as he trod around the wooden floor of the Tower. He told me that he had come to Ireland alone for the sole purpose of visiting places associated with Joyce and Beckett and also to listen to traditional Irish music. He was staying in Page's Guesthouse in Capel Street, which was run by an old Jewish major retired from the British Army. They had long conversations late into the night over some Guinness and Power's Whiskey. Magnus and his Danish wife, Tineke Daalder, the well-known illustrator, later visited Dublin on many occasions, and welcomed me when I went to Gothenburg in May 1993 to give a lecture and to meet with members of the James Joyce Society of Sweden and Finland. The occasion of the lecture was the launching of the re-issue of the Swedish edition of *Ulysses (Odysseus)* by Bonnier Alba.

Richard Ellmann called a few times and we corresponded frequently. I thought that a book about Joyce's connection with the Tower written by him would be a good idea, and would sell well. Ellmann agreed to write it. It was entitled *James Joyce's Tower, Sandycove, Co. Dublin*. I helped with the research and provided the maps, graphics and many of the photographs. It was published in 1969 by Hely Thom and is now a collector's item. I called to Oliver D. Gogarty's home on Earlsfort Terrace to obtain a photograph of his father, Oliver St John Gogarty, for the book. He had a substantial library with interesting unpublished photographs of his father, W.B. Yeats and AE. He told me that Chenevix Trench and his father bought a Canadian canoe and used it on the sea when they were staying out in the Tower.

Fritz Senn arrived in July and remained for over two weeks. He stayed with my family in Churchtown. As usual, he brought material for the Tower; this time it was photographs of the Milton Hebald sculpture of Joyce at Fluntern cemetery, and a photograph of Joyce with Paul Ruggiero at the Red Cross Sanatorium, Zurich, which was taken in 1931. During his stay, Fritz had a full programme with a number of social meetings with Niall Montgomery, Eileen MacCarvill, John Garvin, Gerard O'Flaherty and others. He was always in great demand with Dublin Joyceans. We visited 2 Millbourne Avenue, Drumcondra, the home of the Joyce family in 1894, which is described in *A Portrait of the Artist as a Young Man*. The owner, Mr Kelly, informed us that he would be interested in selling the house to someone who would open it as a Joyce Centre. The house was demolished in 1999 after much protest from people both at home and abroad. With Donagh MacDonagh, we went to Michael Scott's house beside the Tower to hear a tape Fritz had recorded earlier at the Zurich Bloomsday celebrations. Unfortunately, the equipment was faulty and we never heard the tape! I took Fritz, May Monaghan and Eileen Veale to visit Clongowes Wood College where Father McErraught SJ welcomed us; we then went to see Donagh MacDonagh's play *Happy as Larry* in the Lantern Theatre. Afterwards, we travelled to Seville Place to link up with the film crew who were shooting the *Nighttown* scenes there. We left after midnight, but Fritz remained to observe the activity, and walked many miles back to our home in Churchtown at dawn. Fritz was svelte, fleet of foot and very fit, and never suffered from fatigue!

In September 1966 I took my holidays, and visited New York. May Monaghan, always thoughtful, sent me a Bon Voyage card, which read, *Wishing Vivien a happy holiday! Love May*. It was a memorable occasion to meet Frances Steloff again. She gave me a great welcome at the Gotham Book Mart, where the oldest Joyce Society in the world was founded. She took me to a swish Italian restaurant where we had a vegetarian dinner, and then went to a Spanish dancing show on Broadway. On our way there, we passed by a few mounted police; she had sugar in her pockets for the horses, which she gave them. Frances was full of life, and I really enjoyed her company. She introduced me to Mary Ellen Bute, producer of the film *Passages from Finnegans Wake*, made over a nearly three-year period in 1965–7, and a recipient of a Cannes Film Festival award. Mary Ellen brought me to see the newly released movie, *Who's Afraid of Virginia Woolf?*

Professor William York Tindall, whom I had met at the Tower earlier in the year, and his wife, invited me to their lovely apartment in New York. We then went to Columbia University to the Men's Dining Club, where we had lunch with Kevin Sullivan – author of *Joyce Among the Jesuits* (1958) – and Lionel Trilling, and discussed Joyce and Matthew Arnold. Trilling was writing a critical pamphlet on Joyce, which he said would give a new slant on Joyce's works. Tindall told me to pass on his regards to Patrick Henchy, Director of the National Library, and also to ask Joseph Strick for a ticket for the first showing of *Ulysses*, which he said he would advertise in Columbia University. Tindall taught at Columbia from 1931 to 1971. He nominated Beckett for the Nobel Prize in Literature; Beckett was the 1969 laureate. Tindall's book *The Joyce Country* (1960) contains some remarkable photographs of Dublin and of places now gone, such as the Nelson Pillar, the Crampton Memorial and Waterhouse's clock. He also wrote *A Reader's Guide to James Joyce* and *A Reader's Guide to Finnegans Wake*.

When I returned to the Tower for the last few weeks of the season, Nathan Halper from New York called with Patrick Henchy. I was also delighted to meet Marjorie Barkentin again when she called. She later sent me a signed copy of Marianne Moore's poems *Tell Me, Tell Me, Granite, Steel,* and *Other Topics*. It bore an inscription from Marjorie:

> In memory of the tour of the Tower and our lovely day together with May, Eileen and your gracious self,
> 25 November 1966.

On 8 December, May Monaghan sadly died. We had known each other for a short time but had formed a firm and loving friendship. She had many friends from all over the world, and was always charming, generous and humorous. She and Eileen Veale were great friends and enjoyed many happy days in each other's company.

CIE Tours agreed to include the Tower on the itinerary of its new Minstrel Tour, which was a literary tour of Dublin. This operated between April and October and added 3,701 to the number of visitors. Visitor numbers were 3,756 and, with the addition of the Minstrel Tour, came to a total of 7,457, a big increase on the previous year.

My article outlining the aims of the Joyce Museum was published in the *James Joyce Quarterly* Vol. 3. No. 4, 1966. I received a letter from Philip Lamar Graham saying, 'your article in the *James Joyce Quarterly* was very interesting and informative and answered several questions I had about who exactly runs the Tower'.

Some visitor comments for the year 1966 included:

'Don't you have a restroom here?'
'There is much more here than at Thoor Ballylee.'
'Thought you would have more on Gogarty.'
'Never realised you had so much.'
'Is this all you have?'
'Your museum is extremely well laid out.'
'You sure seem dedicated.'
'It is so nicely kept, nice and clean and tidy.'
'You are certainly no slouch.'
'Thank you enormously.'

## ~ 1967 ~

The start of 1967 was frantic with correspondence from Fritz Senn, Bernard Benstock, Clive Hart and Tom Staley. The communications were about the exciting preparations for the First International James Joyce Symposium to be held in Dublin. The idea of a symposium was first mooted on 15 January to Michael

Gorman, the Publicity Manager in Bord Fáilte, when Senn wrote to him: 'As you will see from the letterhead there are some plans afoot. The editor of the *James Joyce Quarterly* and I have thought a Joyce Symposium on or before Bloomsday in Dublin would be worth trying. The idea is to have good papers read by Joyceans, to have some discussion and to finish it all with a luncheon.' Mr Gorman replied with an offer of help with publicity: 'if you would send me an outline of your plans whenever they become more firm'.

In the spring of 1967, John Berryman, the American poet, arrived with a photographer named Spencer from London, who took over a hundred photographs of Berryman in the Tower. I was sitting at my desk and Berryman asked me what I was reading in *The Dublin Magazine*. I replied, 'A poem by Rivers Carew.' He asked me for the book, then proceeded to the centre of the room where he stood, book in hand, and read the poem aloud. As he commenced, a group of people from the Dublin Literary Bus Tour entered. There was a hushed silence as they stood around enthralled, listening to Berryman. They thought that it was part of a show put on for their benefit. When he realised he was doing so well with his performance, he then read some of Yeats's poems from another book which was on my desk. Everyone was delighted and when he finished, there was loud applause.

John Braine, the novelist from Yorkshire who wrote *Room at the Top*, also called, accompanied by two reporters, and they remained for the whole afternoon. In his broad Yorkshire accent, he said that, as far back as he could remember, the green hills of Ireland were as familiar to him as the moors of the West Riding. He knew far more about his Irish ancestors than his English ones.

## A Personal History of the Joyce Tower and Museum

His grandmother's father was a Sligo tenant farmer who was dispossessed from his farm for sheltering evicted tenants. Braine said that he had been a librarian in Bingley, Yorkshire, and advised that it is best not to write your first novel before the age of forty. He kindly sent me a ticket for the film of *Ulysses* at the Academy Cinema One in Oxford Street, London. After the film, I met him at the Arts Theatre in Great Newport Street, and he took me to dinner in the Pickwick Club. Before leaving me to the air terminal to return home, he bought me a large chocolate soda! He later sent me copies of all his books, which he had signed. Braine returned to Dublin on 15 June 1971 to feature in a film about his life for the BBC series entitled *One Pair of Eyes*, which included the Tower. I assisted the crew with various film locations in Dublin and County Wicklow.

Ben Forkner, an enthusiastic student from the University of North Carolina, often popped in. He was staying in Dublin, and he and a friend had two huge, powerful motorbikes. I always knew when they were coming because I could hear the two bikes roaring at great speed along the coast road. They would come to the Tower for the afternoon and discuss the state of world literature at great length, and then hare off again at breakneck speed. Forkner, who was later Professor of English and American Literature at the University of Nantes, and then Angers, in France, published three books on Audubon and edited a number of books including *Modern Irish Short Stories*, *A New Book of Dubliners* and *Louisiana Stories*. He also edited *Selected Stories of Benedict Kiely* and was a good friend of the writer.

On 1 March, Richard Ellmann phoned, inviting me to meet him in the Shelbourne Hotel. We met in the lobby, and he told me to call him Dick. We sat in the lounge and talked at length about Joyce, Yeats, Thoor Ballylee and the *Ulysses* film. I brought my personal copy of his biography on Joyce with me for him to sign. He inscribed:

To Vivien Veale the Danai in Joyce's Tower
from one of its sentinels with all good wishes and
affectionate greetings
Richard Ellmann     Dublin 1     March 1967

Ellmann said that he was flying to Zurich the following day to meet a Harvard professor, and that he would be working in Yale the following year. I accompanied him to buy some flowers for Seán O'Faoláin's wife, Eileen.

On 24 April, Fritz Senn sent a draft of the programme for the First James Joyce Symposium (later to become the International James Joyce Symposium) by express mail. The programme was appropriately printed at Dollard's Printing House. It looked smart, with a photograph of the bronze figure of Joyce in Fluntern cemetery on the cover. I dispatched 350 programmes to France, Belgium, Holland, Switzerland, all of Scandinavia, Australia, Canada and the United States. I also sent 300 copies for distribution from other sources, namely the University of Tulsa, Kent State University, and universities in England, Scotland and Wales. The First James Joyce Symposium was sponsored by the *James Joyce Quarterly* of the University of Tulsa, Oklahoma;

## A Personal History of the Joyce Tower and Museum

*A Wake Newslitter* of the University of New South Wales, Australia; *The Dublin Magazine*, Bord Fáilte and the Eastern Regional Tourism Organisation Ltd.

The First International James Joyce Symposium lasted for two days, 15 and 16 June, and more than seventy-five Joyceans from fourteen different countries participated. On behalf of the Eastern Regional Tourism Organisation, I had the title of Organising Secretary of the Symposium, and so wasn't working at the Tower for the duration. In the weeks beforehand, I organised accommodation in hotels, guesthouses and bed & breakfast places around the city. Some participants had grants; others paid for themselves. I dealt with the registration process on 15 June in the Gresham Hotel. There was a queue of people waiting to be checked in and I typed each name on a little card for ID purposes. There was a great gathering of people. Many of them already knew one another, and if they didn't, they certainly would have corresponded with one another. I had already met some of them. It was like one big family.

Among the Irish attending were Peter Costello, Brendan Duddy SJ, Michael Gorman, Felix Hackett, Dr Maurice Harmon, Professor J.B. Lyons, Dr Eileen MacCarvill, Professor Roger McHugh, Niall Montgomery, Gerard O'Flaherty, Dr Lorna Reynolds and Eileen Veale. Guests of honour were Mr Giorgio Joyce and his second wife, Asta, and Mr and Mrs Frank Budgen. The English painter and writer Budgen lived in Zurich and was a friend of Joyce; he wrote *James Joyce and the Making of Ulysses*, which was published in 1934. In a letter to Bord Fáilte, Giorgio wrote, 'I am looking forward to returning to my father's home town after 40 years, and to taking part in the symposium.' Padraic Colum, on behalf of the Irish Academy of Letters, presented a bronze death mask of Joyce to Giorgio. The mask was cast from the original death mask. Before the presentation, Colum, who was two months older than Joyce, reminisced about the time he met James Joyce on a street in Dublin. Joyce had been away for some time, and on this visit, he had his little son Giorgio with him. Colum continued, 'Then – and this is the tragic and solemn part – Joyce told me that the publishers were not going to publish *Dubliners*. It had been suppressed completely for some mysterious reason that nobody has ever found out. There he was, standing on the street outside – the man who was to make his name synonymous with this city – in a desperate state, not knowing where to turn and not knowing where to go. He went over to London.'

Before the official opening, there was a *Finnegans Wake* tour arranged for the previous day, 14 June. Participants met early to take one of two buses due at Bachelors Walk. Gerry O'Flaherty was the guide in one bus, and I took the other. One of the buses was forty minutes late, which caused a lot of frustration, as we were anxious to get going. The windows on my bus did not open, except for that next to the driver's seat. Before leaving the city, the bus got very hot and Umberto Eco became quite troublesome, standing up and giving out about the heat. I politely told him to please sit down, that I had no control over the temperature, and I could stop the bus and he could get out if he so wished. He decided to remain on the bus and sat down without further ado! His book *The Name of the Rose* (1980) later launched him to literary fame.

*A Personal History of the Joyce Tower and Museum*

We paused at 41 Brighton Square, which has a plaque commemorating the birthplace of James Joyce, erected and paid for by Montclair State College, New Jersey, on Bloomsday 1964. We passed by the Yellow House in Rathfarnham, with its Joyce associations, and headed up the narrow, winding road to the Featherbed where we encountered John Huston wearing overalls and a baseball cap shooting the film *Sinful Davey* around a derelict stone house. The actors included John Hurt, Robert Morley, Nigel Davenport, Fionnula Flanagan and Donal McCann, amongst others. They were all in period costume. There were wagons and highwaymen dotted around the mountainside. It was great entertainment. After all the excitement, the bus arrived at Clongowes Wood College, where the chestnut trees were in full bloom and the grass was lush and green. The beauty of the place was intoxicating. Father John Looby SJ, an expert on *A Portrait of the Artist*, greeted us at the door and brought us around the school, but told us to be quiet because the students were doing examinations. The tour ended at the square ditch, after which we thanked Father Looby and travelled on to Chapelizod. We saw the ruined distillery, where John Stanislaus Joyce once worked, Mullingar House, which was Earwicker's pub, and the house by the churchyard, before entering the Phoenix Park, where the passengers got out to stretch their legs at the Wellington Monument. Eventually we reached Howth Castle and climbed halfway up the hill, through the thickets of spectacular pink and white rhododendrons. On finishing the tour at Bachelors Walk, there was a break, until we met again at 8.30 p.m. for a reception at the Silver Swan, Burgh Quay, now sadly demolished!

On 15 June, Dr Roger McHugh welcomed the symposiasts to the first academic session, which included six lectures. Sidney Feshbach, a distinguished professor from the State University of New York at Stony Brook, made history. He was the first person to give a lecture at the first ever James Joyce Symposium. Since then, there have been twenty-eight symposia held in various locations throughout the world. Feshbach's lecture was entitled 'Joyce's Search for an Anglo-European Language.' An *Irish Times* reporter summed it up: 'He set the ball rolling, dealing in particular with the influence of Ben Jonson on Joyce as exemplified in the degree of control which he had in his writing even in the moments of greatest emotion. The "English Style," he suggested, was the basis for Joyce's development of the European language, of his "decision to absorb Europe".'

Professor Margaret Solomon, from the University of Hawaii, then spoke on 'The Phallic Tree of *Finnegans Wake*'. One newspaper reported that a 'mid-western lady professor used language which had never before been employed by either sex in the corridors of the Catholic University College'. Another paper reported that it would neither be wise nor fair to attempt to summarise the content! There was a dinner that evening in the Gresham Hotel. I was seated at the top table with Frank Budgen, Giorgio Joyce, Tom Staley, Bernard Benstock, Gerry O'Flaherty, Francis Warner and Milton Hebald.

In *The Irish Times* the following day, Quidnunc [Seamus Kelly] wrote in his column: 'In the Aberdeen Hall yesterday morning I heard somebody ask: "Have they begun to sympose yet?" The answer speedily given was "By the look of some of them, they're ready to desympose at any moment." He continued, 'Which was really less than fair. In the jungle war of Joyce-scholarship you need to be pretty sinewy to survive, with deep breathing exercises necessary every morning if you're to get ahead of the rest with your chosen quotes from "Finnegan".'

On Bloomsday itself, a very hot day, there were six lectures and a panel discussion in the morning, followed by lunch at the Gresham Hotel where Umberto Eco spoke. I didn't get to hear many of the lectures because the phone was going non-stop. Then there was a tour, which included a visit to the Martello Tower. It really was a historic occasion as Giorgio and his wife, Asta Joyce, were included in the group. At the entrance to the Tower at the top of the iron staircase, David Ward, Harold Naylor and Tom Staley greeted them. I recall the occasion vividly; the quizzical expression on Giorgio's face when he entered the gloomy interior, as if he was wondering what it was all about. He was aged sixty-two at the time and bore a striking resemblance to his father, having the same slim figure and being the same height. He wore thick-lensed glasses, carried a cane, and wore rings. His steel-grey hair, matching the colour of his moustache, was brushed back off his forehead. He looked debonair, being smartly attired in a white shirt and navy blazer with brass buttons.

After the symposium, a number of people wrote to say how much they had enjoyed it. Selected comments included: 'There was something for every taste, and a great deal of everything ... well, shall we say that the weather was hot, and the going was heavy, and leave it at that? It was worth coming all the way from Canada ... Lecture upon lecture about commas and semicolons were delivered by men who otherwise seemed reasonably sensible ... Inevitably there were some humourless folk at the symposium, but the majority of the participants were pleasant scholarly people ... May this be only the first of a succession of Bloomsdays to be remembered ... *Une chose est déjà acquise: Le second Symposium aura lieu en 1969, toujours à Dublin* ... Looking around me now, I remember my grandmother saying that Jim had said to her: "When I am dead they will raise a monument to me."

The First Symposium in June 1967 led to the creation of The James Joyce Foundation (now The International James Joyce Foundation). Giorgio Joyce was appointed as the honorary director; the honorary trustees were Frank Budgen, London and Umberto Eco, Milan. The names drawn up for the Board of Trustees included Jacques Aubert, Bernard Benstock, Mogens Boisen, Clive Hart, Richard M. Kain, Gerard O'Flaherty, Derrick Plant, Jean Schoonbroodt, Fritz Senn, Thomas F. Staley, and Francis Warner. The executive secretary was David Ward; the librarian, George Leinwall, and I was appointed the European Secretary, from 1967 to 1969. It was something of an anti-climax after the symposium was over, but the summer and autumn continued to be busy.

In September 1967, Joseph Liss, writer of *The Benny Goodman Story*, called to the Tower. He was great fun and we had an interesting discussion about jazz. My brother Tom Veale played the clarinet, so I knew something about the topic. It was exciting to meet with Mr Liss from the swing era! He insisted that our photograph be taken on the steps leading up to the Tower.

On 17 October, which proved to be a memorable day, Zack Bowen from the State University of New York phoned me, and we met the following day. Zack was someone you would certainly never forget. He was a larger-than-life character with personality plus, and had a great sense of humour. He had a beautiful singing voice and was an expert on the music and songs in Joyce's work; his book *Musical Allusions in the Works of James Joyce* was published in 1974. After his visit to the Tower and the usual Joyce tour of Dublin, we went to the United Arts Club in Upper Fitzwilliam Street where we met the actor T.P. McKenna, and the artist Patrick Collins, who had donated Joyce's monogrammed wallet to the Tower. A discussion followed on the theatre in Ireland, where Zack said a few words on the subject, and then sang some Irish songs. When he had finished, he was loudly applauded – what a wonderful voice he had. Eileen MacCarvill then entertained us in her elegant home in Fitzwilliam Square.

During the year several offprints, pamphlets and books were added to the library, the most valuable being a first edition of *Finnegans Wake*, generously presented by Professor Roger McHugh of University College, Dublin. Milton Hebald, the American sculptor who was responsible for the bronze statue of Joyce commissioned by the City Council of Zurich to mark the grave of Joyce and his wife Nora, kindly donated a very fine plaster cast of the head of the statue to be a permanent exhibit at the Tower. At the beginning of October, I cleared the Tower completely of all artefacts, and left them in the Dublin Regional Tourism Organisation in O'Connell Street for winter storage. The number of admissions to the Tower increased to almost 8,000 in 1967, and of this number, well over 3,000 were brought to the Tower as part of the Minstrel Tour.

~ 1968 ~

Most of April was taken up with the reorganisation of the Tower for the season, and reinstalling the collection.

A small celebration was held at the Tower on Bloomsday. Brendan Duddy SJ came out early to lend a hand and hoist the Milesian flag. Fritz Senn spoke on 'Joyce and the Joyceans' and Gerard O'Flaherty gave a multi-level reading from the 'Telemachus' episode in *Ulysses*. Notable among those who attended were John Garvin, Niall Montgomery, Mervyn Wall, Roger McHugh, Eileen MacCarvill, Adrian, Siew and Vivi Youell, Monica Sheridan and Eileen Veale. Also in June, Leo Knuth, a professor of linguistics from Utrecht, and a well-known and popular European Joyce scholar, called and informed me that he had done the Malayan words in *Finnegans Wake*. We went for lunch in a Chinese restaurant in Dún Laoghaire, but he said that he couldn't eat much, as during the war when he was in the Dutch colonies, he was arrested by the Japanese and had been in a prison a camp where the food was dire, which resulted in his bad digestion. I met Leo again at his home in Eindhoven, Holland.

On 8 July, a fuse blew and I was left in darkness. Tom Murphy, a staff member at head office, arrived with fifty choirgirls from North Carolina. They had to grope their way in the darkness up to the parapet, where I gave them a talk in the light of the day. It was certainly not an experience for the poor girls to sing about, when they saw nothing of the inside of the Tower.

More fuse blowers arrived in later in the year when a film crew from an Italian TV station came to the Tower to shoot a

Bloomsday 1954: Brian O'Nolan (Myles na gCopaleen) peering from the front carriage passing the Sandymount Martello Tower on the way to the city.

At the official opening of the Joyce Museum at the Martello Tower, Sandycove, Bloomsday 1962. L–R back row: Sylvia Beach, Mrs Eileen Joyce Schaurek, unknown guest, May Joyce Monaghan, Kathleen and John Garvin; L–R seated: Maria Jolas and Frances Steloff (© Paddy Tutty, Irish Tourist Board).

Reporter speaking with Sylvia Beach at the Martello Tower, Bloomsday 1962 (© Paddy Tutty, Irish Tourist Board).

# james joyce tower
## sandycove

the action of james joyce's ulysses opens in the martello tower at sandycove. over the years this tower has become, to readers all over the world, the chosen symbol, the physical starting point of an odyssey which has changed the course of modern literature.
the tower is now a permanent joyce centre with a display of books, manuscripts, records, portraits and his death mask.

**open 10 - 1 and 2 - 5    (sundays 3 - 6)**
**admission one shilling**

Early notice for James Joyce Tower, Sandycove, giving opening times and the admission fee: one shilling.

Vivien Veale, curator of the Joyce Museum, on the steps of the Joyce Tower in the Eastern Regional Tourism Organisation Limited uniform, August 1965.

Cover of the First James Joyce Symposium programme. The symposium was held in Dublin in 1967.

The First James Joyce Symposium programme, showing sponsors, speakers, and order of events: on Bloomsday, there were cocktails at noon.

Padraic Colum presenting Giorgio Joyce with the death mask of his father James Joyce, at the First James Joyce Symposium, Dublin, June 1967. L–R: Mrs Asta Joyce, Giorgio Joyce, Padraic Colum and Donagh MacDonagh (© Irish Tourist Board).

Giorgio and Asta Joyce being met at the entrance of the Tower. L–R: David Ward, Harold Naylor, Tom Staley, Giorgio Joyce and Mrs Asta Joyce (© *The Irish Times*, 1967).

Joseph Liss, who wrote *The Benny Goodman Story*, with Vivien Veale on the steps of Joyce Tower, September 1967.

The English novelist
John Braine with
Vivien Veale (left)
and Dorothy
Stainforth from the
BBC, 1967.

Arthur Power (on
the left) and David
Ward in the Joyce
Tower at the opening
of the Italo Svevo
Exhibition,
October 1969
(© G.A. Duncan).

Vintilla Horia admires the view from the Joyce Tower, Sandycove, 1969 (© Paddy Tutty, Irish Tourist Board).

Milo O'Shea, who played the part of Leopold Bloom in the film *Ulysses*, with Vivien Igoe on the parapet of the Joyce Tower in 1969 (© Paddy Tutty, Irish Tourist Board).

Vivien Igoe presenting a photograph of Joyce's wife, Nora Barnacle, to Robert Nicholson, to mark the hundredth anniversary of Nora's birth in 1884 (© Dermot O'Shea, *The Irish Times*, 1984).

Joe Joyce, author of *Off the Record* and Vivien Igoe, author of *James Joyce's Dublin Houses & Nora Barnacle's Galway*, at the launch of their books in the Joyce Tower, 15 June 1990 (© Joe St Leger, *The Irish Times*).

documentary. They blew every fuse in the place and I was left again sitting in the dark for the rest of the day. A less destructive visitor to arrive was Saul Field, the Canadian artist, who presented a portrait of Joyce.

On 17 July Arthur Power, a most interesting friend of Joyce, and author of *From the Old Waterford House* (1940) phoned and said he would like me to call to his house, which I did. He gave me the manuscript of a book he had written on Joyce to read and comment on. It was later published as *Conversations with James Joyce*, edited by Clive Hart (1974).

August visitors included Frances Steloff, who visited Dublin again. Together with Eileen Veale, we went to the Abbey Theatre where we met Tomás Mac Anna, Director of the National Theatre. Other August arrivals were a remarkable trio who called to the Tower. Included were Harry Levin, professor of English at Harvard, author of *James Joyce: A Critical Introduction* (1941); Leon Edel, the American author and critic, who wrote a five-volume biography of Henry James; and Professor Heinrich Straumann from Zurich who told me that he had interviewed Joyce in Zurich shortly before his death on 13 January 1941. The same day an American visitor called and bought two copies of *Ulysses*. After the purchase, he passed the books back to me and asked me if I would do him a favour and please sign the copies. I politely reminded him that I did not write *Ulysses*, but he insisted nevertheless that I sign them! I obliged without further ado.

August 1968 showed a small glimmer of hope concerning the acceptance of Joyce in Ireland. An international summer course lasting two weeks, entitled 'James Joyce, the Artist and the Man', was organised by Noelle Clery, Director of the Language Centre of Ireland. She was certainly a woman ahead of her time, and started the ball rolling for foreign students interested in studying Joyce in Dublin. I put up a poster in the Tower advertising the course, which was held at Wesley College, St Stephen's Green. It was attended by fifty students of Joyce from Holland, Spain, France, Germany, Italy, the French Cameroons and Israel. Initially, all the lecturers were Irish and included Dr Grattan Freyer, Fr Brendan Duddy SJ, Augustine Martin from UCD, Dr John Garvin, Dr John de Courcy Ireland, Gerard O'Flaherty, Irish Trustee of the Joyce Foundation, Eoin O'Mahony, Dr Eileen MacCarvill, Gerard Lee and Charles Acton. A highlight of the students' course was a visit to the Tower, where Gerard O'Flaherty briefed them on the 'Telemachus' episode. This was the first year the Language Centre of Ireland had organised such a course; it proved so successful, it became an annual event, moving to the centre's headquarters at 5 Wilton Terrace, Dublin 2, with international speakers such as Leo Knuth, Clive Hart and Richard Ellmann giving lectures. I also lectured at the summer school.

In early September, Ulick O'Connor, accompanied by Sarah Churchill, visited the Tower. Sarah was the daughter of Winston Churchill and was a dancer and actress. William J. Clew, the managing editor of *The Hartford Courant*, visited the Tower for the first time in September. He had Irish ancestry and a great love for Ireland. He became a lifelong friend and published all the news releases and features which I sent him. He was acquainted with Padraic Colum, and kept me updated on him, especially during Colum's final years. Later, Professor Walshe from UCD called with Sonia Orwell, the widow of George Orwell, accompanied by Pablo Picasso's agent. They spent some time looking around the Tower and admired the view from the parapet. Sonia was blonde, good-looking and extremely charming. She told me she had been born in India and educated at the Sacred Heart Convent in Roehampton, so we had that in common as I was educated at the Sacred Heart Convent, Mount Anville! We got on very well together.

The season closed on 30 September 1968. Well over 9,000 people had called since May, which was a major achievement. All the items in the display cases were packed again into boxes, labelled and moved into an empty room in the Dublin Regional Tourism Office, O'Connell Street.

~ 1969 ~

The year got off to a wet start when in January it was discovered that the Tower was reeking with damp.

Investigations revealed some of the timbers in the floor were rotten and liable to collapse. A damp course specialist was called who gave an estimate for repairs. That's as far as it got! The start of the year was busy planning for the Second International James Joyce Symposium to be held in June. A lot of time was taken up with correspondence. All the letters had to be typed, then franked, and finally posted. Some took days to arrive at their destination. Then there was a lapse before the replies arrived. There were no emails in those days. I spent time in the National Library researching old documents and papers to answer queries, and preparing for the symposium. In May, the Tower opened for afternoons only because of the dampness and uninhabitable conditions. The admission charge was increased by 100 per cent from one shilling to two shillings. I suggested the increased revenue should be kept to finance a complete damp-coursing job to be carried out as soon as we closed for the winter.

April, May and the first half of June were taken up with pre-symposium activities, mostly related to marketing the project. I dispatched over 300 copies of the final programme to likely participants, sent out a press release to all the newspapers, arranged accommodation for symposiasts, left posters in relevant places, and dealt with publishers concerning a book display planned for the Moyne Institute, Trinity College. Bord Fáilte Éireann, the Eastern Regional Tourism Organisation, *A Wake Newslitter*, and the *James Joyce Quarterly* sponsored the symposium, presented under the auspices of the James Joyce Foundation. It was held from 10 to 16 June 1969 at Trinity College. About 130 people attended the opening. The guests of honour were Mr and Mrs Frank Budgen and the chairmen were Bernard Benstock, Fritz Senn and Tom Staley, with co-chairmen Gerry O'Flaherty and Niall Montgomery from Dublin and Maciej Slomczynski from Poland. Slomczynski, the Polish translator of *Ulysses*, presented a copy of his translation to the Tower. He was a celebrity in his country both as a translator and writer of crime fiction.

The number of participants who registered for the symposium was 234, with the largest number from the United States. This figure represented a sizeable increase on the previous symposium held in 1967. The wide-ranging programme included academic sessions, panel discussions, Joycean tours, and a book display of

*A Personal History of the Joyce Tower and Museum*

Joycean publications from all over the world. There was also a social programme which included the European premiere of *Night Boat From Dublin*, a new play based on the letters of James Joyce, presented by Harry Pollock. This was staged at the Peacock Theatre with a cast of Abbey Theatre players. A Joyce exhibition, held at 50 Mountjoy Square, included drawings, paintings, etchings, engravings and sketches, featuring the work of artists from Copenhagen, London, New York, Paris, Trieste, and Dublin. Mrs Desmond Guinness and the Irish Georgian Society kindly lent the house for the exhibition.

The opening session of the symposium took place at the Moyne Institute at Trinity College Dublin where the provost of the College, Dr A.J. McConnell, welcomed the attendees. Tom Staley introduced the first speaker, Elgin W. Mellown, Duke University, North Carolina who spoke on 'Joyce's Sense of Order and Its Value to the Twentieth Century'. Richard Ellmann's book *James Joyce's Tower* had just been published. Along with Noel Carroll from the Eastern Regional Tourism Organisation, I presented a copy to the Provost of Trinity College.

I took fifty of the symposiasts on a four-hour tour on Bloomsday. Starting from Trinity's 'surly front', we journeyed to Glasnevin cemetery via all the places connected with *Ulysses* on the way. Pausing outside 7 Eccles Street, the Joyceans stared at the half-demolished building in disbelief. It would amaze some prosaic citizens to know the horror aroused in foreigners by the destruction of Joycean landmarks in Dublin, such as this house. Eventually we reached the Tower, and after a visit to Mr Deasy's school in Dalkey, we returned to the city.

Jack Dalton, the textual scholar from Canisius College in Buffalo, NY, was also a speaker at the symposium. He arrived out to the Tower on a bike. He was in the habit of saying and doing things that nobody else ever did, or thought of doing. He wrote a letter to *The Irish Times* complaining about bits of rubbish that had gathered on the floor of the large water feature in the Garden of Remembrance in Parnell Square and suggested that an underwater vacuum cleaner might be used to clean it up. He stayed in a guesthouse, and the owner rang me to say that Dalton had left the tap running in the handbasin in his room. The water had leaked down through the ceiling, flooding the place. The owner then demanded to know what was I going to do about it. I told him I wasn't a plumber and that the water leaking down through his ceiling had nothing whatsoever to do with me. Mr Dalton had booked himself into the guesthouse, so he could sort it out with him!

I was privileged to meet Professor Mabel Worthington from Temple University, Philadelphia, on 18 June. She was perhaps the first Joycean to hone in on the musical elements in Joyce's works and collaborated with Matthew Hodgart with a book, *Song in the Works of James Joyce* (1959). She became a great friend, stayed in our home, and travelled with my mother to visit Lucia Joyce in Northampton. Father Bob Boyle SJ, from Marquette University in Wisconsin, stayed for a while, and called to the Tower on 1 July. We went to the Harbour Master's house to enquire about the currents in Dublin Bay: it was in relation to the body washed up in the text of *Ulysses*. Other callers that autumn included Szemethy Imre, who did the illustrations for the Hungarian

*A Personal History of the Joyce Tower and Museum*

translation of *Ulysses*. Vintilă Horia, the Romanian-born writer who had an extraordinary life, and won the Prix Goncourt in 1960 for his novel *Dieu est né en exil* (God was born in exile) arrived, armed with his tape recorder. He read from *Ulysses* sitting on the gunrest on the parapets. I brought him around the usual haunts, and we had a meeting with Bozena Delimata, Joyce's niece, at her home, where Vintilă met Finn – his first Irish wolfhound.

On 30 August, the postman delivered a bundle of letters Amongst them was a circular from *Time* magazine addressed to 'Mr James Joyce, Museum, Sandycove, Dublin, Ireland.' Its circulation department kindly offered to send copies of the magazine to Mr James Joyce at a reduced rate of one shilling provided he ordered a minimum of twenty-five copies. In September the postman called again, this time with a letter from Nelly Joyce, widow of Stanislaus, who lived in London. She wrote:

> I have an upright piano that belonged to James Joyce during his stay in Trieste, which came in my possession through my late husband, Stanislaus Joyce. I now wish to dispose of it because I am moving to a smaller house, but I would very much like it to remain in the hands of people who would care for it as an historical object. Miss Jane Lidderdale suggested to me the James Joyce Tower may be interested in keeping this piano: it is in good condition and I feel it would be an interesting item in your collection.

> I would be obliged if you would indicate whether you are interested.
>
> I remain,
> Yours faithfully,
> Nelly Joyce

Having already acquired Joyce's guitar for the collection, I was delighted and replied to Mrs Joyce to accept her kind offer. On 27 October she wrote that 'the piano is at present in London, at a friend's house: I would expect the Joyce Museum to bear the cost of transport from London to Dublin. I am informed by a local removal firm that the cost is in the region of £25 door to door, plus insurance. The piano itself, of course, is a gift. I trust that your special exhibition at the Tower is a great success.'

Shortly afterwards I received a postcard from Miss J.H. Lidderdale OBE (former guardian of Lucia Joyce), which read:

> I am so glad you like the idea of having the Joyce piano. And I hope it will like the idea of being so close to the sea! It may need tuning rather often, perhaps? Anyway, I hope Mrs Joyce will have it sent to you before long, now she is settled in her new place. *Dear Miss Weaver* is to be published next Autumn, by Faber and Faber [It was being finished just at the symposium time]. The friend [Mary Nicholson] I got to help me with it, I have made joint author.
>
> Best wishes for the New Year.
> Jane Lidderdale

## A Personal History of the Joyce Tower and Museum

The piano duly arrived but, owing to the humidity in the Tower, it was stored elsewhere – besides which, it could not have been carried into the Tower through the narrow entrance at the top of the iron staircase. Later, when a ground-floor entrance was created, it remained in the Tower for twelve years before being transferred to the Dublin Writers Museum, where it stayed for the next thirty years, apart from a year in the James Joyce Centre, 35 North Great George's Street, following the piano's restoration. It is presently in the dlrLexIcon Library in Dún Laoghaire.

To coincide with the Dublin Theatre Festival of October 1969, I organised a special exhibition at the Tower entitled '*Ulysses* in Italy'. The Italian Institute was helpful in providing information. The exhibition featured copies of Joyce's letters to Italo Svevo (the pseudonym for the Triestino writer Ettore Schmitz), who was Joyce's pupil at the Berlitz School in Trieste. It also included maps, photographs and a display of Svevo's works; Joyce's works in Italian and recent criticism of Joyce and Svevo; together with hitherto unpublished photographs of Svevo, as Joyce knew him; several postcards and nine letters. Dr John Garvin, Dublin City Commissioner, opened the exhibition and gave a witty talk on the Svevo/Joyce relationship in Trieste. It was one of the most successful functions ever held in the Tower since 1965 with Arthur Power, Seamus Kelly, and the press present. The inimitable Milo O'Shea, who acted the part of Leopold Bloom in Joseph Strick's film version of *Ulysses*, visited the Tower just before it closed for the winter. He spoke about his interesting life as an actor and his experience of playing the part of Bloom in the film.

At the end of October, the contents of the Tower were removed and stored in dry accommodation for the winter months, and I went to work in Head Office at Moran Park.

~ 1970 ~

On 1 May, the Tower opened for the season.

On Bloomsday morning, a hot day, I did a live broadcast at the RTÉ Radio Centre, then based in Henry Street, on *The Liam Nolan Hour*. I subsequently returned to the Tower to get things organised for the Bloomsday lecture. I had contacted Chalmers (Terry) Trench from Slane, Co. Meath, to give a talk on Dermot Chenevix Trench. He protested and said he was not a Joycean and knew nothing about Joyce. I said, 'But you do know about Dermot Chenevix Trench.' He said he didn't, but he could find out. He said that Trench was a third cousin of his father. True to his word, he did the necessary research and gave a most entertaining and informative lecture on Bloomsday entitled 'Dermot Chenevix Trench, a guest in the Tower in 1904.' Terry remarked that it was entertaining partly because he found fault with the pundits, including Richard Ellmann! The audience liked his lecture, and I persuaded him to write it up and have it published, which he did. It later appeared in the *James Joyce Quarterly*, Vol. 13, No. 1, 1975. The guests at the lecture included many Joyceans such as Bozena Delimata, John Garvin, J.B. Lyons, Eileen MacCarvill, Ken Monaghan, Niall Montgomery, Michael Scott, Eileen Veale, Bea Orpen (Mrs Trench) and Seamus Kelly (Quidnunc), who reported the event the following day in his *Irish Times* column. Gerry O'Flaherty, courteous as always, sent a telegram from Shannon Airport. 'Apologies but can't make it tonight. Have a good meeting and a Happy Bloomsday.'

A wonderful opportunity presented itself when Michael Scott's house 'Geragh' came on the market. Since 1965, repairs, such as pointing the brickwork, had been carried out on the Tower. However, because of the sea air and heavy winter rains, the Tower was proving an unsatisfactory place to house the valuable collection, even though it was removed for the winter months. Fungus had developed on pictures and paintings, and original manuscripts were curling up with the damp. After six years, it was time to take action. Michael Scott was willing to sell his house next to the Joyce Tower, which offered plenty of space, for £30,000. To convert it into a museum, library, meeting rooms, lecture area, toilets and restaurant would cost a further £20,000. I wrote and circulated a comprehensive plan in late 1969 concerning the purchase of the house and the benefits of establishing a Joyce Centre next door to the Joyce Tower. It was the perfect solution.

During 1970, exploratory meetings commenced and continued regularly throughout the year, with members of the James Joyce Foundation, the Eastern Regional Tourism Organisation, and Bord Fáilte attending. At the meetings, plans were discussed to buy 'Geragh' and set up a Joyce Centre, which would attract Joycean scholars and tourists from all over the world. David Ward put a tremendous amount of work into the project on behalf of the James Joyce Foundation, together with Noel Carroll and myself on behalf of the tourism organisation. Fritz Senn, Bernard Benstock, David Ward and George Leinwall travelled from abroad to attend the meetings.. Articles appeared in national and international press, often carrying headlines such as 'Hopes for a New James Joyce Centre'; 'ERTOL plans a Joyce Centre'; 'Now is the time to re-Joyce'; 'Goldmine in the Tower'.

On 29 October I removed all the contents and books from the Tower for winter storage.

~ 1971 ~

Sadly, 1971 would prove to be a year of frustrations on the infrastructural side, but it did have its literary compensations ...

In early spring, Professor Masayoshi Osawa, the first president of the James Joyce Society of Japan, visited the Tower. He liked Irish culture so much that he spelt his name O'Sawa. He was a frequent and popular visitor to Ireland over many years, with his wife Kaoru. O'Sawa's translation of *A Portrait of the Artist as a Young Man* was later published on Bloomsday in 2007. With a few exceptions, the Joyce Tower was closed to visitors for the whole of the 1971 season due to its condition and continual problem with dampness. It was now unsuitable for housing staff and displaying exhibits; these were left in storage for safekeeping. The Eastern Regional Tourism Organisation called on Bord Fáilte to help finance the renovation, but Bord Fáilte was short of funds and considered that the Tower was not its problem. The continued closure proved even more embarrassing when the international PEN conference took place in Dún Laoghaire. Ichiro Ando, who had translated *Dubliners* into Japanese, could not gain access to the Tower, along with many other luminaries. There were numerous complaints to the press, with headlines such as 'Writers find

Joyce's Tower locked' and 'Architect demands opening of the Joyce Tower'. Mr Scott, the architect who bought the Tower in the fifties, added that he was very disappointed with the closure. He had sold it to the tourism body at the price he originally paid – on condition it would be kept open on an ongoing basis.

Another even more caustic press headline read, 'Joyce Tower – Nobody's Child'. And yet another, 'Three bodies say no to appeal'. The accompanying text read: 'Although the Tower has been attracting thousands of visitors annually and generating untold amounts of positive international publicity, neither the Eastern Regional Tourism Organisation, Bord Fáilte or Dún Laoghaire Borough Corporation, is prepared to put up the necessary funds to reopen it.'

While lack of finance was the main reason for the prolonged closure of the Tower, other factors included the fact that staff refused to work and stay there because of the cold and damp; the lack of sanitary facilities for themselves and for visitors; and the fact that the floor had begun to show signs of dangerous wear and tear.

In the midst of a pervading sense of gloom, meetings continued concerning our plans for the purchase of Michael Scott's house. I made an attempt at fundraising to buy the house, and opened a bank account, but the contributions were small, and I ended up returning the cheques received. Saul Bellow, the American novelist who was awarded the Nobel Prize for Literature in 1976, was one of the contributors. Had the house purchase initiative been realised, the resulting Joyce Centre would have incorporated a library, and would have become the focal point of the world's most important Joyce collection.

I had first met George Leinwall at the Joyce Symposiums in 1967 and 1969 and had been his guest in the United States. A retired civil servant from Randallstown, Maryland, he offered to donate his entire Joyce library, the largest private collection in the world, to the Tower. This unique treasure trove included more than 1,000 first-edition volumes of Joyce works that he had collected over the years. He was prepared to spend some months each year acting as honorary librarian to the collection. This was just one example of what might have been achieved. Desmond Rushe, columnist in the *Irish Independent*, wrote: 'the only thing that will prevent it coming here is cheeseparing lunacy in official quarters. The combined forces of Bord Fáilte, Eastern Region and Government failed to do anything. Not a finger was lifted to secure for Joyce's country the greatest collection of Joyceana in existence. And offered to us free.' The collection, which was on offer for two years, was later sold to the Southern Methodist University in Dallas, Texas. This was a national tragedy and a terrible loss to Ireland. It was a huge disappointment for those of us who had fought for so long and negotiated so hard. I was absolutely appalled that an opportunity to acquire this magnificent collection was lost to the nation. I did what I could, but to no avail. It was time to fold up my tent, and silently steal away.

Later in the year, Thomas J. Keating, a Dublin businessman who had a roofing and restoration firm, generously offered to restore the Tower at his own expense. The Eastern Regional Tourism Organisation accepted the offer, and the work proceeded. The first priority was to restore the original floor. Two-inch oak had to be cut out specially to overlock in the old way and span

## A Personal History of the Joyce Tower and Museum

the twenty-five-foot diameter of the main room. The trapdoor in the centre of the floor was reconstructed to align with an old iron ring in the ceiling by which ammunition was once lifted on a pulley from the artillery store in the basement. The floor was sanded and sealed. Louvred wooden blinds were inserted into the small slanted windows; masonry was re-mortared where draughts penetrated the walls, and the whole interior was painted in white acrylic paint to retain warmth and prevent dampness. A hole was drilled in the base of the wall, and forty gallons of old rainwater was emptied from a seam. A rim was added to the top stair to form a shallow catch basin and eliminate another source of damp, and lighting was installed in the winding staircase. Paddy Robbins, one of the workmen, said, 'It was an awful job, the dirt and cold in the place was very bad.' However, no facilities were added for the comfort of the staff or tourists.

On 26 November 1971, my days with the Eastern Regional Tourism Organisation ended. I moved to Bord Fáilte as an editorial publicity officer, but continued to work with Joyce Tower matters for some time. Since my new job involved dealing with overseas writers and journalists, I had many more opportunities to visit the Tower where I gave occasional lectures, and where my book *James Joyce's Dublin Houses & Nora Barnacle's Galway* was later launched in 1990.

### ~ 1972 ~

The restoration work at the Tower was completed just after the fiftieth anniversary of the publication of *Ulysses*, which took place on 2 February.

In March, I returned all the museum exhibits and books and set up the Tower for the 1972 season. On 16 June, a plaque was unveiled commemorating Mr Keating's restoration of the Tower. The honour was well-deserved. Shortly afterwards, I met James T. Farrell, the American author, who was in town visiting his friend, the writer Ben Kiely. Farrell, author of fifty-four books, including the *Studs Lonigan Trilogy*, was anxious to visit the Tower, having earlier written about Joyce. He was mischievous and had a great sense of fun. We headed off on a tour during which he recounted his rough-and-tumble boyhood in lower-middle-class Irish-American life on Chicago's south side. He was proud of the fact he was one of fifteen children, born in the auspicious year of 1904. For whatever reason, Farrell carried his portable typewriter with him. After spending some time in the Tower and admiring the view from the summit, it was time to head back. In all my years working in the Tower, there was never an accident with either young or elderly people falling on the iron stairway leading up to the entrance. This was about to change.

On the way out, having locked the door, I led the way. Farrell followed with his typewriter tucked under his arm, and stumbled on the stairway. Fortunately, I caught him and broke his fall. Farrell claims I saved his life! Partly as a result, we became the best of friends. He sent me copies of all his books signed, and an invitation to New York to stay for as long as I liked. His book *Reflections at Fifty* (1954) contains a long chapter on 'Joyce and Ibsen'.

It is time for me to close this chapter of my years as Curator of the Joyce Tower. I was privileged to have covered those early years and was fortunate to have met and corresponded with friends of James Joyce and most of the early Joyceans. I was certainly in the right place at the right time! *Quid multa?* as Cicero says. Need I say more?

VIVIEN VEALE IGOE
September 2023

# THE FURTHER HISTORY 1972–2019

*Robert Nicholson,*
*curator*

~ 1972–8 ~

Following Vivien Igoe's departure and the work to the building funded and carried out by Tom Keating, the museum reopened in 1972.

Between then and my appointment as curator in 1978, the museum was served by a succession of short-term curators who opened the museum to visitors during the season.

Nora Goodbody was the first short-term curator. She responded to queries, welcomed visitors and looked after the collection. Denis Bates worked in the museum in 1975, carrying out a similar range of curatorial duties. Roland McHugh served as curator from 1976 to 1977. In addition to being an authority on entomology and on grasshopper acoustics, Roland was already a prominent Joyce scholar and a member of the small band of pioneers who were gathering together glosses and annotations for *Finnegans Wake*. His personal account, *The Finnegans Wake Experience*, briefly mentions his appointment and time at the Tower, describing it as 'tolerable enough except for the tourists ("James Joyce? Who's he?").' He ensured that some of the world's more useful works on *Finnegans Wake* were added to the museum library and in due course contributed his own, *The Sigla of Finnegans Wake*, and his monumental *Annotations to Finnegans Wake*.

The early 1970s saw the establishment and growth of a solid base of Joyce readers and scholars in Ireland, a phenomenon that was not confined to the universities or to literary circles. The James Joyce Institute, now Ireland's longest-running Joyce society, was set up to hold occasional public lectures and conduct regular reading sessions, mainly devoted to *Finnegans Wake*. Vivien Igoe and Roland McHugh were among the members. David Norris from Trinity College was making his name as James Joyce's chief publicist in Ireland with colourful lectures, entertaining performances and readings and a determination to present Joyce as a writer for everyone to appreciate and enjoy. He organised the return of the International Joyce Symposium to Dublin in 1977, an event in which the Eastern Regional Tourism Organisation, owners of the Tower, were involved.

By now the owners had particular plans for the James Joyce Museum. The proposal to take over the neighbouring property, although now abandoned, had succeeded in concentrating minds on the constrictions of the Martello Tower as a museum building. Designed to keep people out rather than welcome them in, the Tower's first-floor entrance and steep staircase were a challenge to visitors, the domed living-room was still nearly as gloomy as it is in *Ulysses* (and limited in space), and the lack of a toilet was a test of staff endurance.

*A Personal History of the Joyce Tower and Museum*

Michael Scott and his son Niall, working with Scott Tallon Walker Architects, were engaged to design a ground-floor extension that would complement and blend with the tower and its surroundings. Standing as it does on a granite knoll with the ground quarried away steeply on all sides, the tower had only a limited curtilage within which to position the new building. The architects worked within these limitations to design a quadrant-shaped structure whose outer wall followed the curve of the Tower itself and the similar curves on Michael Scott's house next door, the battery over the Forty Foot and the piers of Sandycove Harbour. A glazed screen was fitted at the front and back, and the boundary wall facing onto the path was removed to create an open aspect looking out across the bay towards Howth.

Visitors approaching up the path were now welcomed with a front door at ground level and the opportunity to look through the window before coming in. The outdoor stairway, dating from the 1940s, was removed and the original front door now opened onto a drop of about a metre to the flat roof of the new building. The ground floor inside the Tower was opened up with a new doorway leading in from the extension, and the redesign included a staff toilet and a small kitchen and storage area. The changes necessitated removing the old magazine chambers with their partition walls and covering up the ground-floor fireplace, which is now buried in the space between the toilets and the kitchen. The gunpowder magazine was fitted with lights and became an additional exhibition space on the route from the entrance hall to the spiral staircase.

## ~ 1978 ~

In May 1978, when I became Curator of the James Joyce Museum, building was still in progress.

The work had been slowed down by the laborious task of cutting the new opening through the tower wall, with its outer shell of solid granite and its rubble core. As the months went by, it became clear that the museum would not reopen that year. Instead, I spent the rest of the year working as a supernumerary and general assistant in the Eastern Regional Tourism head office in Dún Laoghaire. I also spent whatever time was available becoming familiar with the background history of the museum and with whatever of its contents I could get at in the storage room in the office basement. As part of the homework, I began reading back numbers of the *James Joyce Quarterly* from the museum library in search of useful information. I soon formed a picture of what was then known as 'The Joyce Industry' and who its leading lights were. Not all the articles were outstanding, but I gradually gravitated towards those writers who dealt in fact rather than theory.

Summer moved into winter and what had started as a seasonal position was extended indefinitely, eventually to become a permanency which was to remain with me for another forty years.

## ~ 1979 ~

By spring of 1979 the building was ready for occupation, and the furniture and other contents were returned to the premises.

I also inherited Annie the cleaner, who retained her heretical opinions on Joyce's occupancy. A new arrival on the scene was the Antonín Petrof piano, which James Joyce had bought in

## *A Personal History of the Joyce Tower and Museum*

Trieste in 1906 and that had stayed there in 1919 in the possession of Stanislaus Joyce when James moved to Paris. Stanislaus's widow Nelly had donated it to the museum when she moved to London, but it had remained in care for some years until the creation of a ground-floor entrance made it possible for it to be brought into the Tower.

Another striking item, and the first I added to the collection, came from Samuel Beckett, to whom at the suggestion of a friend I wrote asking if he would come and perform the official opening of the extension. He did not accept, but to my excitement his reply came in a package containing a red, yellow and blue tie and a card, which read:

> Dear Mr Nicholson,
> Thank you for your letter of March 23 and for your kind invitation which to my great regret I cannot accept.
>
> My best wishes for an auspicious inauguration of the new building. Long may it stand and inspire.
>
> The enclosed tie was given to me by Joyce in 1929 or 1930, from his large store of ties. Perhaps it once went with the waistcoat.
>
> With all good wishes.
> Yours sincerely                                Samuel Beckett

To begin with, the collection was displayed in much the same order as before and in the same cases, which were now accommodated inside the new extension. The piano and book collection in the next room shared the gunpowder magazine with the curator's desk. The desk by the front door was used by the seasonal assistant I had been allocated for the summer months, who would look after admissions and give me the opportunity to do business or attend meetings in Dún Laoghaire, Dublin or elsewhere. The round room upstairs was now empty, apart from a few pictures, and the idea was that it could be used for talks, readings and other events with the aid of a supply of stacking chairs which were arranged around the walls.

The museum reopened at the beginning of May 1979 and we spent a few weeks settling everything into place before having the official opening at the end of the month, attended by a mixed gathering of Joyceans and tourism worthies. From here it was just a short hop to the seventy-fifth anniversary of Bloomsday. By present-day standards this was a modest affair, and if the day's visitors were aware of the date at all, they were content to mark it by paying homage at the newly reopened museum without all the additional rituals of straw hats and kidneys, singing, reading and drinking which are now associated with 16 June. To mark the day, however, I had arranged a special evening at the Tower. John Ryan and Anthony Cronin reminisced about the first Dublin Bloomsday celebration in 1954 and John showed his memorable home movie of the event. The other special guest was Lennie Collinge, former projectionist at the Volta cinema, who was probably the only person still alive who remembered meeting Joyce in Dublin. The occasion was a memorable one and quickly demonstrated both the atmospheric nature and physical limitations of the round room as a venue. We persevered with the evening events, which included a lecture by David Norris, a talk on Oliver Gogarty's birthday by his biographer Ulick O'Connor, and dramatised readings of 'The Mookse and the Gripes' from *Finnegans Wake* and 'The Cat and the Devil', the story Joyce wrote for his grandson Stephen.

A week of events in September to celebrate the seventy-fifth anniversary of Joyce's stay in the Tower featured not only a birthday cake for Molly Bloom's 109th birthday but also readings from *Ulysses* by Eamon Morrissey which he would later bring to the stage under the title *Joycemen*. Denis Johnston gave a lecture on *Finnegans Wake* and there was also a talk by Professor Declan Kiberd.

Although the museum closed for the season at the beginning of October, I continued to open it by appointment, since it was no longer considered necessary to move the contents of the museum into storage for the winter. These appointments often involved visitors with a particular interest in Joyce rather than casual tourists visiting the local sights, and at this quieter time of year I was able to give them personal tours and attention. Now that the extension was up and running, it had been decided to continue the work by replacing the old display cases with new ones, and the winter was spent looking at designs and quotations. Conscious that the museum had no back office or storeroom, I asked for the cases to be built with cupboards in the base, though I had no idea at the time how useful they would become.

## ~ 1980 ~

The beginning of 1980 also started the countdown towards the Joyce centenary of 1982.

A committee was set up to organise the International Joyce Symposium, with its programme of public events. As before, the tourism organisation was involved and provided office services, and I was asked to reprise Vivien Igoe's role as secretary of the symposium committee. David Norris chaired the committee (which, to most intents and purposes, also served as the official committee for all the centenary celebrations), and a wide range of academics and cultural figures was brought in to take part. As with most such committees, some of these merely added decorative lustre to the proceedings, some provided help and connections as needed, and a smaller core did most of the hard work. One of my early duties was to make a visit to Paris, partly to do some hands-on familiarisation and research and partly to bring news of the plans to some of Joyce's surviving friends and acquaintances.

Samuel Beckett, who was very courteous, signed the Tower's copy of *Our Exagmination Round his Factification for Incamination of Work in Progress*, the 1929 collection of critical essays on *Finnegans Wake* and related some personal memories of Joyce. Maria Jolas entertained me in her apartment, and Gisèle Freund gave me English tea and recalled Sylvia Beach's vexation at Joyce's habit of extracting money from her and then bestowing it lavishly on the first beggar he met in the street. Nino Frank told me the inside story of the *Déjeuner Ulysse* in 1929 and how he and Samuel Beckett came not to be in the official photograph (unlike Philippe Soupault, whom I also met). Joyce's grandson Stephen gave me his views on the Joyce industry, and Paul Léon's son Alex met me in the family flat on the rue Casimir-Périer, where Joyce had written much of *Finnegans Wake*. On a visit to London, I took the opportunity to visit Jane

## *A Personal History of the Joyce Tower and Museum*

Lidderdale, goddaughter of Joyce's great benefactress Harriet Weaver. As receiver for Lucia Joyce, Miss Lidderdale arranged for me to have a meeting with Lucia in the hospital in Northampton. While these encounters did not involve material for the museum collection, they established a link with the actuality of Joyce's life and added to the experience for visitors by putting them at only three degrees of separation from Joyce himself. My notes on my Paris encounters were to come in useful to Seán Ó Mórdha, the filmmaker who was then preparing his documentary on Joyce, *Is There One Who Understands Me?* for RTÉ.

The museum reopened for the season in May. It was an occasion to welcome a new and significant addition to the collection. Following an approach from a private seller and with the help of a sponsor, the museum was able to acquire a first edition of *Ulysses* – number 819 of the 1,000 copies published, in its original blue-and-white cover – to display in the building which it had made famous. The volume had already played its part in Joyce scholarship, having been used as a reference copy by one of the team working on *The Corrected Text of Ulysses* (of which more later). It was given a case of its own among the suite of new display cases designed for the museum, and retains its central importance in the collection.

Bloomsday was quiet enough, with an unremarkable sixty-six visitors. Eamon Morrissey was premiering *Joycemen* at the Peacock Theatre that evening and I did not arrange anything to clash with the performance. Later in the month, we hosted a series of musical performances given by singer Treasa O'Driscoll. Treasa and her husband Professor Bob O'Driscoll from Toronto had many connections with the Dublin cultural scene and attracted a star-studded audience. They were also involved in the visit in July 1980 by the *Marques*, a sailing barque chartered by the charismatic Richard Demarco for Edinburgh Arts to make a cultural voyage of discovery around Britain and Ireland. The ship had recently starred as the *Beagle* in a BBC TV series about Charles Darwin's voyages, which added an extra dimension to the project. An evening visit to the museum with special entertainments was planned for the mariners and their guests, and at the last moment I was asked if they could use the building for a party afterwards. Culture had little to do with punctuality and everything ran very late. I did a short slide show; Treasa O'Driscoll performed; John Ryan showed his film of Bloomsday 1954; and the sculptor David Nash, who happened to have a film in his pocket, requested the use of the projector and the audience while they were still in situ. The party went on until one o'clock in the morning, and when I had finished clearing up, I went round to Michael Scott's next door to join a few of the lingering revellers. John Ryan, Paddy Collins and Micheál Ó Nualláin were seasoned late-night talkers and I didn't get home until 3 a.m.

The Tower acquired unusual prominence in the ROSC International Art Exhibition in Dublin in 1980 when a replica of the building was constructed in Earlsfort Terrace by the Argentinian conceptual artist Marta Minujín using 5,000 loaves of bread (donated by Downes's bakery). Once complete, the structure was turned on its side and dismantled, and the loaves of bread were thrown to hungry art-lovers and representatives of charitable organisations.

## ~ 1981 ~

I was equally as busy outside the museum as within it, raising its profile through association and involvement in meetings and cultural activities across Dublin and communicating with prominent figures in the Joyce industry.

Richard Ellmann, who came out to the Tower during a visit to Dublin in January 1981, was characteristically charming and provided copies of Joyce's and Nora Barnacle's letters written at the time of the Tower episode. A talk by Alec Reid to mark Samuel Beckett's seventy-fifth birthday in April 1981 attracted a closely packed audience of seventy-five into the round room. Other lectures and evening events continued, augmented by a slideshow of pictures of Joyce's Dublin from the Lawrence Collection, which was to become a regular feature. Numbers, however, could be very unpredictable and on some occasions there would be a mere half-dozen in attendance.

Bloomsday, for all that it attracted its quota of devotees, was still a quiet enough occasion, marked only by its own luminescence. The sixty-six visitors on Bloomsday 1980 doubled to 132 on Bloomsday 1981 (though seventy of them belonged to a school group who had come to the Tower as a second option after finding their planned destination in Dún Laoghaire closed). As 1982 drew closer, the museum – still the only centre dedicated to Joyce in his native city – became a focus for those researching books, documentaries and commemorative projects. One of the first off the block was Frank Delaney, who launched his handsome book *James Joyce's Odyssey* at the Tower in the autumn of 1981. Interspersed throughout the book with period photos of Joycean

Dublin were contemporary images by Jorge Lewinski. His photo taken in the entrance hall to the museum shows the walls still almost bare of pictures – a situation that was soon to change.

Not all my enquiries, however, were strictly scholarly. As I recorded in my diary for 23 September:

> That afternoon, the telephone rang. 'Is that 809265?' asked the operator. 'I have a call for you.'
>
> 'Hello,' said a strong American female accent at the other end of the line, 'is that Mr Jawce?'
>
> 'Uh, no,' I gasped, 'my name is Nicholson.'
>
> The lady was only momentarily nonplussed.
>
> 'Oh well, is your wife's name Jawce?' she demanded.
>
> 'No, no,' I gurgled desperately. 'I'm not married.'
>
> Visitors to the Tower were already beginning to fold up.
>
> 'Is Mr Jawce there?' persisted the caller.
>
> 'He is not,' I assured her, '– uh, perhaps …'
>
> 'Is that the Jawce Tower James?' she asked.
>
> 'This is the Joyce Tower,' I spluttered, 'but I …'
>
> 'Is there *anyone* there called Jawce?' she asked, despairingly.
>
> 'This is a museum,' I said firmly – 'it's named after a writer who died forty years ago. I am the curator.'
>
> The penny began to descend.
>
> 'Aw – well, mah family were Jawces, they came over from Ireland during the last century – Ah thought you might know something about them …'
>
> 'But the Joyces came from Galway,' I put in.
>
> 'Well, Ah was told that, but ah thought you'd know more.'

As the pips were pipping, I advised her hastily to consult Bord Fáilte or the Genealogical Office.

## ~ 1982 ~

The events of 1982 transformed international awareness of Joyce and brought his works out of the academy and onto the streets.

The Irish contribution was particularly notable. The year kicked off with announcements of the plans for the centenary year and the upcoming symposium at a reception attended by the writer Anthony Burgess, who was in town with a BBC crew and working on a musical adaptation of *Ulysses* named *The Blooms of Dublin*. (I had dinner with him in The Bailey afterwards and walked home in the snow because the last bus had departed).

I was not present on 2 February, as I was enjoying a new-found emissary status as a speaker on Joyce at the celebrations in Trieste and had travelled there with Kieran Hickey, who was presenting his film *Faithful Departed*. The locals, who told me they had expected the museum curator to be 'an old man', were nonetheless welcoming and included Italo Svevo's daughter Letizia, whom I met at the unveiling of Joyce's bust in the public park. Thanks to the work and enthusiasm of John McCourt, who arrived there a few years later, Trieste is now a Joyce hub with its own summer school, James Joyce Museum and walking tours. The talk in Trieste led to another one in Bologna in March, but from then on everything built up towards the major celebrations in June.

In addition to my work on the centenary committee, I took to the streets to familiarise professional tour guides with a *Ulysses* walk through the city centre, delivered a portrait to Clongowes so that Joyce could finally join their gallery of famous past pupils, and answered innumerable queries. The effects on the museum were considerable, not only with regard to increased visitors and public awareness, but also in terms of new items for the collection. There was a boom in new (and in several cases important) publications about Joyce and translations of his works – many of which were given as complimentary copies for the Tower library – and a surge in commemorative artworks and Joyce-related merchandise (the good, the bad and the ugly).

Aer Lingus commissioned a limited-edition print by Louis le Brocquy based on Joyce's death mask and presented one to the museum at the artist's request. Centenary medallions arrived from Dublin, Trieste and Zurich. More unusually, a recording by Danny Doyle of Shay Healy's song 'Finnegan Are You Really Dead?' was presented in a frame. *Ireland of the Welcomes* published a Joyce centenary number, including a special article on the museum, which I was asked to write. The issue was launched at the Tower in May.

One original piece of Joyce memorabilia was a copy of John Ruskin's *Mornings in Florence*, signed by a youthful Joyce in September 1898 and acquired when he was studying for his UCD matriculation exam. The owner, who had discovered it in a box of books in his house, offered it on sale to the museum and the money to buy it was kindly provided by Lucia Joyce through the offices of Jane Lidderdale. Another significant addition was the first issue of Samuel Roth's infamous *Two Worlds Monthly* containing the opening of the pirated publication of James Joyce's

*A Personal History of the Joyce Tower and Museum*

*Ulysses*, and Samuel Beckett sent a further gift of two of the Faber fragments of *Work in Progress*, one of them signed to Beckett by Joyce 'with thanks for his help' (the inscription was also placed and dated 'London, 10. v. 1931', which linked it to Joyce's residence there at the time of his wedding).

On Bloomsday itself, the Tower was selected by RTÉ as one of the public broadcast points for its thirty-hour dramatised recording of the whole of *Ulysses*, which could be listened to in the museum throughout the day. Most of the public events, however, were taking place in the city, and once the museum was up and running for the day, I slipped into town to witness the unveiling of the bust in St Stephen's Green and to play a small part in the historic staging of the entire 'Wandering Rocks' episode on the locations and at the times specified in the novel (under the title *O Rocks!*). In the role of the Reverend Hugh C. Love, I put on a frock coat, a clerical collar and 'a refined voice', and was escorted through the chapterhouse of St Mary's Abbey by candlelight, while a short distance away a huge crowd was converging on the Ormond Hotel to avail of pints at 1904 prices. Up in North Great George's Street, the keys were being handed over for what would become the James Joyce Centre. For the rest of the week, I shuttled between symposium events and my duties at the museum, where there were visits by international Joyce scholars and countless journalists representing every aspect of the media.

The Centenary Symposium was the biggest and most distinguished to date and attracted scholars from all over the world, giving me the opportunity to connect with some of the most respected figures in the Joyce industry. Richard Ellmann was there, and so was Clive Hart, whom I had already met on the occasions when he left in copies of his excellent *Topographical Guide to Ulysses* for sale at the Tower. Clive took the part of Father Conmee in *O Rocks!* and somehow wound up on Ormond Quay where we were photographed together in our respective clerical garments. Hugh Kenner was present to unveil a plaque on Leopold Bloom's supposed birthplace in Clanbrassil Street. Fritz Senn, whom I met for the first time at the symposium, was someone I was to meet on many more occasions during his regular visits to Dublin. The groups he brought with him from Zurich would visit the Tower, go on walks through Joyce's Dublin or have joint reading sessions with the James Joyce Institute. Also present were Pieter Bekker, Alistair Stead and Richard Brown from the University of Leeds, who in 1980 had set up *The James Joyce Broadsheet*, a thrice-yearly periodical of Joycean news, reviews and illustrations, and had asked me to become their Dublin News contributor – a position which, somehow, I have held ever since.

Not all my activity at the symposium was connected with administration and I was invited to be a panellist in a discussion on Joyce Collections. It was led by Willard Potts, who had just edited a book of recollections of Joyce by Europeans, *Portraits of the Artist in Exile*, and the panel also included Myra Russel, who would keep in touch with me about her work on Geoffrey Molyneux Palmer. The symposium and other centenary events achieved their objectives of placing Joyce in the public consciousness and of establishing Dublin as the essential pilgrimage centre for all Joyceans – a place where they came to learn rather than to teach.

## A Personal History of the Joyce Tower and Museum

Every new book or documentary or photograph collection about Joyce's Dublin featured the Joyce Tower, and its iconic shape became well known in pictures and posters. Not unnaturally, there were more visitors and more people for whom their arrival at the museum was a special moment. Meanwhile, the small sales stand at the entrance to the Tower, which had previously been populated by a few postcards, copies of Joyce's works and some books about him, was now overwhelmed by new books, posters and Joyce-related merchandise, and the selection and control of stock became a growing feature of my curatorial duties.

~ 1983 ~

While comparatively restful, 1983 brought further additions to the collection.

Nora Barnacle's niece Patricia Hutton, whom I had met at her home in London in 1980, travelled to Sandycove to present the museum with James Joyce's cabin trunk, a sturdy container decorated with Joyce's initials and labels from his European travels. The trunk had accompanied Joyce to London at the time of his wedding in 1931 and he had given it to Nora's sister, who had brought it back to the family home at Bowling Green, Galway. A few splashes of candle-grease suggest that it had spent its time under a bed with one end projecting as a stand for a bedside light. It returned to London with Nora's brother Thomas, who left it to his daughter. Meanwhile a photographic exhibition on Joyce and Trieste, which had been mounted for the centenary by the Italian Cultural Centre, was presented to the museum when 1982 was over. It not only filled a Trieste-sized gap in the museum displays but also took the bare look off the walls of the round room upstairs.

There was already enough material in the museum to provide the makings of another slideshow, this time tracing Joyce's life through documents and museum objects and providing viewers with an opportunity to go beyond the limits of what could be displayed in the museum showcases. I gave it the title '*The Haunted Inkbottle*', not only in reference to the shape of the building but also because the museum was already beginning to resemble Shem's house in *Finnegans Wake*, with random objects scattered all over the floors and walls.

After the events of the centenary year, Bloomsday was beginning to attract public attention. To help create a festive atmosphere at the Tower, some of the principal founder members, such as Michael Scott and John Ryan, were invited in to mark the twenty-first birthday of the museum with champagne and speeches. An unusual gift on the day was the door of the gunpowder magazine, which had been removed by the builders from the Tower during the recent alterations and had become part of the decor in Nora Barnacle's Restaurant in Dún Laoghaire Shopping Centre, where I discovered it. Although the doorway it had occupied was no longer there, the restaurant owners kindly agreed to return it to the museum to stand against the magazine wall. Another significant event of the day involved Joycean Michael O'Kelly, who arrived at opening time with a Primus stove, a frying pan and a kidney and proceeded to cook a Bloomsday breakfast al fresco, thus marking a custom that would grow out of all recognition in the years to come. He had explored the possibility of cooking it indoors but, quite apart from fire safety considerations, I had visions of 'the fine tang of faintly scented urine', as noted by Leopold Bloom in Chapter 4, lingering throughout the building for the day.

~ 1984 ~

The centenary of Nora Barnacle's birth on 21 March 1984 received less attention than her husband's had done, but the day was marked at the museum by the presentation of a portrait photo donated by Vivien Igoe, who gave us a lecture on Nora later in the year.

Another lecturer that year was American scholar Grace Eckley, who was determined to present her claim that the newspaperman W.T. Stead was not just a pervasive presence in *Finnegans Wake*, but an actual original for Earwicker in the novel.

Behind the scenes I was occupied by a certain amount of repair and maintenance work (the new extension had not altogether solved the problem of keeping the building warm and dry); the installation of a security alarm (to keep up with the times); and by the redesign of the *Ulysses* Map of Dublin to replace the original version produced by the Joyce Tower Society in the 1960s. I took the opportunity to plot in a few more locations and mark the routes of Paddy Dignam's funeral and the viceregal cavalcade, and even went so far as to propose expanding the whole thing into a booklet with more detail about the itineraries of each episode. The budget was not available for a booklet and we stuck with the map.

Building on the publicity that Bloomsday had attracted the previous year, I issued a press release encouraging visitors to dress up for the day and to read extracts from *Ulysses* as appropriate. For the occasion, Vivien presented us with another photograph from her seemingly inexhaustible store, showing Joyce in his flat in Trieste with, in the background, the same piano that now stood in the museum. The principal presentation that day, however, was the first copy of the three-volume *Ulysses: A Critical and Synoptic Edition*, published by Garland Press (some hours ahead of its official launch in Frankfurt, which gave us a world scoop). This marked the culmination of years of textual scholarship to correct the countless errors that had been perpetuated and transmitted throughout the entire publishing history of *Ulysses* over the previous seventy years. The new edition, intended primarily for scholars, included not only a final 'corrected' text, but also a page-by-page synoptic view of all the textual decisions that had been made. Danis Rose and John O'Hanlon, two members of the editorial team, got their first sight of the finished publication when they arrived to present it in front of assembled scholars, Joyceans and journalists, and since it was the only copy in the country, it was almost immediately being consulted by those who had been asked to review it. It was another champagne occasion and attracted a certain amount of media attention, especially because at this stage the Tower was still the only location where there was a party atmosphere and the few other events organised for Bloomsday took the form of lectures or formal presentations.

~ 1985 ~

One of the noteworthy arrivals of 1985 was the photograph of Throwaway brought in by a gentleman from Battersea.

## A Personal History of the Joyce Tower and Museum

He had been admiring it with his son in an antique shop when they suddenly realised that this was the same horse made famous by the pages of *Ulysses*. I got some further information from the Newmarket Horse Museum and much later discovered that this was one of three prints presented respectively to the owner, the trainer and the jockey. Another addition to the walls was Eamon O'Doherty's lively set of three prints illustrating episodes from *Ulysses*. For Bloomsday, the now-familiar garden-party outfit involving stripey blazers and straw boaters had become established, as had the early opening (it was 8.30 a.m. then and subsequently moved back to the regulation hour of 8 a.m.) and the traditional shared reading of the opening pages of the book on the roof of the tower as soon as it was open. This was the first year that I engaged an actor, in this case Gerry Farrell from Sligo, to perform extracts from *Ulysses* at intervals throughout the day, and this too was to become a regular feature of Bloomsday at the Tower.

One of the primary duties of every curator is the protection and safe-keeping of a museum's collection of artefacts. Another duty, and one that can occasionally lead to awkwardness and embarrassment, is to ensure that all bequests or gifts made to the museum remain firmly in its possession and not become the assumed property of anyone connected to the museum. In the latter part of 1985, this ethical issue came to the fore. It revolved around the gifting to the museum of a death mask of James Joyce.

At the time of Joyce's death in 1941, Mrs Giedion-Welcker had obtained permission for the sculptor Paul Speck to make two casts of Joyce's face. The idea was that she would have one and the family would have the other, but Nora Joyce was unable to pay for it, so Mrs Giedion-Welcker kept both masks (a third mask was later presented by Paul Speck to the Library of Congress in Washington DC, but it is not known whether it is an original or cast from one of the other two). She gave the mask to Michael Scott for the museum in the late 1950s and photographs were taken of it at the time of the opening.

Perhaps under the impression that the mask was a personal gift, Scott retained the original when the museum later changed hands. He presented the museum with one of two bronze casts or 'pulls' made by Werner Schorman, with the other going to the Abbey Theatre, which had been rebuilt to Scott's design in the 1960s.

I had once asked Michael where the original was, but hadn't received an answer. The matter rested until July 1985 when I had an irate phone call from Stephen Joyce, demanding to know if it was the Joyce Museum that had just put the mask up for auction at Sotheby's.

The proposed sale was taken up by the newspapers, and numerous Joyceans and others added their comments. Ultimately, the sale went ahead, but later it was rescinded and, after some quiet negotiations, the mask eventually came into the possession of the museum, to go on display the following year once a suitable case had been designed, constructed and installed in the gunpowder magazine.

Stephen Joyce dictated the wording of a brief label, which made no mention of Paul Speck or Carola Giedion-Welcker. I managed to credit them by reference in the caption on the bronze copy in the next room. It was a satisfactory ending to an uncomfortable episode.

*A Personal History of the Joyce Tower and Museum*

Relationships with Stephen Joyce were sometimes problematic, and shortly afterwards when the company decided to make and sell Joycean souvenirs – replicas of the Tower key, the blue-and-white tie that Joyce designed as a gift for Paul Léon and bars of 'Bloomsday Lemon Soap' – to raise revenue for the museum, he announced that he had cancelled bequests to us. I was naturally distressed, but had to reflect that it was something that was bound to happen sooner or later for one reason or another and was actually surprised that he had put us on his bequest list at all.

~ 1986 ~

Work on the new case for the mask was just part of the programme for 1986.

The impressive glazing of the 1979 extension was letting in too much light for the prints and manuscripts housed within, so we applied UV film to the windows for the protection of the contents. The back window, however, faced the full glory of the afternoon sun and from an early stage I had taken to leaving down the back shutter. Another consequence of the 1979 alterations was that a draught now came in through the unsealed front door and the new opening in the tower wall and thence through the gunpowder magazine and up the open stairway to the roof, sucking out all the heat and replacing it with cool sea air. The remedy was to add a door at the bottom of the stairs.

A paper conservator came in to work on the condition, mounting and display of some of the items in the collection, and I managed to obtain a larger bookcase for the museum library, which was expanding rapidly, thanks not only to the boost in publications since the centenary, but also to kind gifts of new translations of Joyce's works in more and more languages. A dehumidifier was installed to cope with the ever-present problem of water penetration at weak points in the mortar of the tower walls. Fresh copy prints were made of some of the photographs in the collection and displayed in glass frames on the walls inside the Tower. Some money was also available to buy one of the Orthological Institute recordings of Joyce reading from the *Anna Livia Plurabelle* section of 'Work in Progress' in 1929, which was framed and hung.

The death mask finally took its place in the museum three days before Bloomsday, installed in a secure, specially designed damp-proof display case in the gunpowder magazine. Dan Schiff sent us as a Bloomsday present his print of the opening page of *Ulysses*, showing Buck Mulligan (complete with gold fillings) and Stephen Dedalus on top of the tower, together with the text of the first page. As a display item near the entrance, it meant that anyone who looked at it would at least have started *Ulysses* by the time they moved on into the museum, and for those who couldn't manage the staircase, it gave an idea of what they couldn't see above it. Even the packaging in which it arrived had been so beautifully hand-decorated that I preserved it for the archives.

The other significant Bloomsday event that year was the launch of the popular Penguin edition of *Ulysses: The Corrected Text*, following the appearance of the Garland synoptic edition two years previously. Visitors who bought a copy on the day were treated to a special bookplate certifying that it had been acquired in the Tower on Bloomsday 1986. Without too many rival events,

## *A Personal History of the Joyce Tower and Museum*

we were able to attract the Joycean great and good of Dublin to the launch event after closing to visitors at the end of the day.

The honour of being the first to set off the alarm on the death mask case went to Bob Joyce, who was examining his great-uncle's features too closely, while the honour of introducing Bob to his cousin Ken Monaghan on the same occasion went to me. Both Bob and Ken were to become involved in the restoration and development of a city-centre Georgian house as the James Joyce Centre, a project initiated by David Norris and launched in 1982 when the proceeds of the Joyce Symposium went towards reroofing the building.

As a legacy of my work on the Joyce centenary committee, I had become secretary of the board of trustees of the Joyce Centre as the long work of restoration and fundraising got under way, and I worked to ensure that the roles of the museum and the cultural centre would remain distinct. As the centre built up its profile, I took to reinforcing the use of the official designation 'The James Joyce Museum' for the establishment in Sandycove and using the term 'The Joyce Tower' to refer to its location or address. In addition to maintaining our claim on the title, I felt that it was important to emphasise what we did there and to get away from the idea that it was simply a historic building open as a visitor attraction.

As a member of the Irish Museums Association since 1980, I had developed a great deal of respect for the profession to which I belonged. At its annual seminars I shared ideas and experiences with staff members from large and small museums throughout the country, debated the levels and methods of interpretation when displaying a collection, and subscribed to the universal wisdom that museums should be curator-led.

The museum had always had its share of celebrity visitors, from Betty Friedan and Seamus Heaney to Sarah Miles, Steven Berkoff and Bob Geldof, and Senator Michael D. Higgins had brought his guest Sergio Ramirez, novelist and vice president of Nicaragua. Spike Milligan also made a memorable visit. In June 1986 the first prime minister came to call: David Lange, the New Zealand premier, made a special request to see the Joyce Museum while he was on a State Visit to Ireland. Popular with Irish CND for his anti-nuclear stance, he was greeted by a crowd of local admirers outside the Tower when he arrived and proceeded in a statesmanlike, plump sort of way towards the stairhead. Other dignitaries appeared over the years and I was occasionally asked to host receptions or give tours for visiting foreign ministers and groups of EU delegates.

After some work on the telephone line, I had been able to move my desk out of the gunpowder magazine and had created a little office area behind a display case at the back of the exhibition hall to use when there were two of us on duty. In those pre-digital days, I was still reliant on the Regional Tourism Office in Dún Laoghaire for typing and other secretarial services and frequently had to cycle up there in my lunch hour to collect, sign or deliver material. With an eye to independence, I acquired from the office a cast-off typewriter of Eastern European make, which no longer typed the letter 'a' or the @ symbol but which was otherwise useful for small jobs like labels on exhibits or updating the stock lists. To add to this, I was given a redundant office photocopier which saved me further journeys, but it did take up a lot of space.

*A Personal History of the Joyce Tower and Museum*

## ~ 1987 ~

With occasional money to spend on acquisitions, my next target was to collect first or significant editions of Joyce's works to fill in the gaps in the sequence.

I was fortunate to be able to purchase reasonable copies of *Exiles* and *A Portrait of the Artist as a Young Man* to mark the museum's twenty-fifth anniversary in 1987. The occasion was celebrated on Bloomsday with a rerun of the party we had held four years earlier, and provided an opportunity to welcome back Michael Scott after the embarrassment of the death mask episode. John Ryan had just republished his memoir, *Remembering How We Stood,* and presented me with a copy for the museum library. However, as I ruefully wrote in my diary, we did not possess it for long:

> I found myself facing Michael Scott. Conscious that since we had last met, I had been involved in a campaign to prove misappropriation of property intended for the James Joyce Museum, I put such thoughts behind me and broke the ice civilly.
>
> 'Did you see John Ryan's book?' I said, showing him the latest addition to the collection.
>
> Scott took the book, admired it, and graciously accepted it.
>
> 'Thank you very much, John,' he said to its author, who had appeared beside us.
>
> He then walked off to talk to someone else, and the book went with him: I stood up again to introduce John Ryan who read us the appropriate passage from his oeuvre.

George Morrison, whose photograph of the opening of the museum is significantly the culminating image in his book *Ireland – the Emergent Years*, lent me a few prints for the occasion and revealed that he had also made a film record of the opening, which was still in his garden shed waiting to be edited.

It had already been a busy Bloomsday. Inspired by reports of Michael O'Kelly and his like frying up their Bloomsday breakfasts outside the Tower, local restaurateur David Byrne of the South Bank restaurant on the seafront decided to make an event of it by opening early in the morning to serve inner organs of beasts and fowls, made palatable by draughts of champagne and other alcohols to wash it down. He conferred with me about the menu, the music and other suitable accompaniments and I suggested he should fly the Greek flag in homage to the cover and themes of *Ulysses*. I was not then aware of what we had unleashed on future generations of Joyceans, but it made a great spectacle in the early morning sunshine with celebrants assembling in their finery and the odd horse and carriage pulling up outside.

The James Joyce Centre, which had yet to make the Bloomsday breakfast its own event, was still at the fundraising stage. Nonetheless, this was the year the Centre introduced the concept of extending the activities into a festival lasting for several days. The administrator of the Centre, Des Gunning, got married to Tina Robinson on Bloomsday and they also managed to be among the early morning visitors to the museum on the occasion.

One of the regular celebrants, a gentleman named Ciaran Daly, was first through the door with a surprising gift for the museum. 'I've got the black panther!' he claimed, depositing on the desk a ceramic piece of giftware representing the animal in question in almost life-size dimensions. Though it could hardly be described as a Joycean artefact, the panther settled down to become part of the furniture and a useful prop in the story of Trench's nightmare. Later that year, the panther got its own cameo role when Donald Taylor Black and Roger Greene came to film their documentary about Oliver Gogarty.

Richard Ellmann, whom I had met and corresponded with on various occasions, died in 1987 and I represented the museum at his memorial service on a wet day in Oxford. Seán Ó Mórdha, who had filmed a documentary with Ellmann, presented a fine photo of him to add to the museum collection.

Other extra-mural activities were less sombre. My proposal to expand the *Ulysses* map of Dublin into a booklet had been shelved for a couple of years before catching the attention of Edwin Higel, who persuaded me to expand it further into a full-length book for publication by Methuen, entitled *The Ulysses Guide: Tours Through Joyce's Dublin*. I spent much of my spare time prowling the streets of Dublin with a notebook to pinpoint the locations of *Ulysses* and relate them to the modern cityscape, gleaning along the way countless nuggets of knowledge with which to regale visitors to the museum and answer their questions.

On a related project, I worked with the sculptor Robin Buick to design a series of pavement plaques following an episode of *Ulysses* through the city centre, with quotations at the appropriate points, under the title 'The Footsteps of Leopold Bloom'. To cover the whole book was too ambitious a task, and we decided to limit ourselves to the closely described and agreeably situated itinerary of the 'Lestrygonians' episode (with a single inclusion for Bloom's final location in 'Aeolus' nearby in Middle Abbey Street). To lend the project a symbolic context, the plaques corresponded in number with the fourteen Stations of the Cross, but possibly the only person to have noticed this was Stephen Joyce, who said it looked like 'some sort of Via Dolorosa'.

~ 1988 ~

The pavement plaques were intended to form part of the celebrations of the Dublin Millennium year in 1988.

This was an occasion that gave rise to events and commemorative projects all over the city and attracted great attention from the world's travel journalists. By this stage, Joyce's place in the national heritage was widely recognised and every travel writer or TV crew that came to Dublin had to do a Joyce story. Independent crews were making documentaries and programmes about Joyce's Dublin and inevitably they all came to the Tower for filming and interviews (mainly in the week of Bloomsday when I was already busy enough). 'The Footsteps of Leopold Bloom' series (represented for the occasion by the plaque outside Davy Byrne's) was unveiled by the Lord Mayor on the morning of 15 June, and the same evening Methuen held a launch party for *The Ulysses Guide* (and the rest of their current Irish list) at the James Joyce Museum. Favoured with fine weather, most of the crowd of publishers, booksellers, journalists and authors congregated outside, with the Tower as a backdrop to the proceedings. I combined the duties of author with those of host, curator and bookseller. When the guests and caterers had finally

## A Personal History of the Joyce Tower and Museum

gone, I stayed to make sure the building was presentable and ready for its early morning opening.

Fortified by the 'Inedible Modality of Thick Snotgreen Giblet Soup' on the South Bank's breakfast menu, I reported to the museum at 7.30 so that the *Arena* crew from BBC could film my arrival on my bicycle, followed by the raising of the flag and the opening of the door for Bloomsday. By mid-morning, they were still jostling with RTÉ and Swiss TV for interviews with me when a delegation arrived from Saint-Gérand-le-Puy to present a portrait of Valéry Larbaud, the French writer who had championed Joyce in the 1920s and had supervised the French translation of *Ulysses*. The Lord Mayor of Saint-Gérand made a formal speech in French to which I was obliged to reply while simultaneously keeping the bemused public aware of what was going on. When they requested that the portrait be displayed immediately, it was fortunate that there was a space on the wall and a hammer and nail to hand. Gerry Farrell came to perform and there were unscripted appearances by Philip Mullen (who shaved on top of the Tower and went on into town to perform 'The Parable of the Plums' in O'Connell Street with the aid of a stepladder) and Nora Connolly, who turned up regularly every Bloomsday, immaculately costumed, to deliver a monologue presenting herself as a character in *Ulysses* or a woman in Joyce's life. Seamus Heaney had the courtesy to wait until the next day to call in with Derek Walcott. (Seamus was wont to entertain Nobel Literature laureates on their visits to Dublin and came in on another occasion with Nadine Gordimer.)

Bloomsday 1988 also saw the beginning of another Dublin Bloomsday institution – the performances by the Balloonatics theatre company of episodes of *Ulysses* on location in walks through the city streets, readings on street corners and in pubs and bookshops. Their activities continued throughout the day and culminated with an evening show named 'Humid Nightblue Fruit'. Afterwards, the floor was opened, daring members of the audience to read, perform or otherwise interpret Joycean passages. Balloonatics regular Paul O'Hanrahan was occasionally aided and abetted by other members of the troupe when available.

This was also the year that the Dublin James Joyce Summer School was founded by Augustine Martin and Terry Dolan. Stephen Joyce turned up and made a surprise visit to the museum to inspect the death mask and comment on the exhibits. He was sitting in the row in front of me at Newman House when I attended Clive Hart's lecture at the opening of the school and he asked a loaded question about 'biographers who make use of distorted memories'. Later he informed me 'I told Professor Martin what I thought of him,' but I politely refrained from asking for details.

The lectures and sessions of the Summer School, some of which I managed to attend, were reported daily in the newspapers. As always, I regularly received visits from passing Joyce scholars and was occasionally able to help them with their research. Myra Russel, whom I had already met at the 1982 symposium, came in one day on the track of Geoffrey Molyneux Palmer, whose settings of Joyce's *Chamber Music* she had uncovered. She had just been telling me about his sisters, the Miss Palmers, who had run Hillcourt School nearby, when two of their former pupils – my mother and her cousin – came up the path and consented to be introduced. They were able to provide Myra with some first-hand memories of the ailing composer in his wheelchair. Although it was not a year for high-profile acquisitions, I was pleased to accept a gift of a battered old French dictionary bearing the signature of John Stanislaus Joyce of 7 St Peter's Terrace, Cabra. Whether this had belonged to James Joyce's father or to his brother was not certain, but I added it to a case of miscellaneous articles, including the Plumtree's pot, a fragment of the Nelson Pillar, a package with F.W. Sweny's label and other curiosities. They would be joined the next year by a Clongowes pandybat which Father Fogarty had discovered in a cupboard.

~ 1989 ~

The pandybat wasn't the only souvenir of James Joyce's schooldays to come our way in 1989.

A gentleman named Brian Ellis revealed himself as the grandson of Joyce's former English teacher George Dempsey (who appeared as 'Mr Tate' in *A Portrait*) and from him we obtained a creased but original Christmas postcard with a message from Joyce as follows: 'To his English master with fond remembrances from his old pupil – James Joyce'. The card was sent in December 1917, a year after the publication of *A Portrait*, which may well have encouraged Dempsey to contact Joyce. It also turned out that Brian Ellis's father had been the Garda sergeant who rescued a frozen Oliver St John Gogarty after his dramatic escape from his kidnappers by swimming across the Liffey. Gogarty had been brought to the police station in a state of hypothermia and was revived with warm blankets. The station ink bottle had been emptied of its contents and refilled from the kettle to provide a much-needed hot-water bottle. Restored to life, Gogarty had presented Brian's father with a personally inscribed gold cigarette case as a mark of gratitude. Another striking addition to the collection was Jan de Fouw's fine print 'Molly B' incorporating the final lines of *Ulysses*, which so appropriately complemented Dan Schiff's print with the opening page that I hung one at each end of the extension wall with Eamon O'Doherty's prints in the middle.

The most significant acquisition of the year, however, had to be the copy of the two essays 'A Forgotten Aspect of the University Question' by F.J.C. Skeffington and 'The Day of the Rabblement' by James A. Joyce. Published in October 1901, it was a joint production by Joyce and Francis Sheehy Skeffington, whose essays had been rejected by the university magazine *St Stephen's* because of their content. Although it is believed that only eighty-five copies were printed, some remained in the possession of Sheehy Skeffington's family and it was from his daughter-in-law, Andrée Sheehy Skeffington, that this was acquired at a special presentation ceremony in August 1989.

The publishers were back for another eve-of-Bloomsday party at the museum, this time to launch Brenda Maddox's biography of Nora Barnacle Joyce. I had some qualms about this, which were borne out a few days later when Nora's grandson rang up to put a flea in my ear. 'Were you not aware of how offensive I find this garbage?' he said of the book (it is well known that Stephen Joyce generally resented biographers).

Bloomsday itself brought more crowds than ever (including Marie Curley who was the first woman to shave on top of the tower). Barry McGovern, who had approached me some time beforehand to discuss the possibility of reading *Ulysses* at the Tower, launched the project with 'Lestrygonians'. On a day when the air would be rent with hundreds of strident declamations of Joyce's masterwork, I knew that it would be our duty to have *Ulysses* properly presented by a master who would do it justice. Barry, who already knew the book well and had studied the episode carefully, read it in three parts over the course of the morning in the sunshine on the roof, where the round gunrest and the firing step provided seats for his enraptured audience.

Outside the bounds of Sandycove, the tourism organisation was keen to contribute to Bloomsday in the city and I was given some funding to organise appearances by the celebrated street artist Thom McGinty, known as 'The Diceman'. I helped to design a costume in which he dressed up as the first edition of *Ulysses*, open with the title page and the schema information for 'Lestrygonians'. The following year he portrayed a map of Dublin with Joycean locations marked on it. I also found time during the year to produce another book, *The James Joyce Daybook*, published by Anna Livia Press, which was essentially a diary for 1990 with Joycean anniversaries marked all the way through and enlivened by entertaining illustrations by Henry Sharpe. The collection of dates was eclectic enough and ranged from the birthdays of Joyce and his family to the occasion on which Leopold Bloom weighed himself 'in the premises of Francis Froedman, pharmaceutical chemist of 19 Frederick street, north'.

~ 1990 ~

Another project I had been working on for some years had been prompted when a visitor to the museum revealed that she was a granddaughter of 'old Troy of the DMP' in *Ulysses*.

'But he wasn't a bit like Joyce described him,' she said primly, no doubt referring to the words 'that old bollocks you were talking to'. Although I failed to act on it immediately, it then occurred to me that it would be good to collect photographs of *Ulysses* characters for the museum and perhaps put them in a book at some stage. I mentioned this to Kevin Myers in *The Irish Times* and he produced a photo of his great-uncle Jack Myers of the Dublin Fire Brigade, recorded as having set fire to Leopold Bloom. A family member sent me a photo of William Brayden, editor of the *Freeman's Journal*, and early in 1990 John Osman gave me two fine photos of Davy Stephens, the famous newsvendor.

Vivien Igoe's book *James Joyce's Dublin Houses & Nora Barnacle's Galway* was launched at the pre-Bloomsday publishers' party in 1990, which also featured a new work by Dublin author Joe Joyce. Joe had no connection with his myopic namesake but later wrote a play called *The Tower*, in which James Joyce and Oliver Gogarty are imagined meeting again in a certain building in Sandycove.

Bloomsday itself continued to outdo its predecessors for crowds, colourful behaviour and craziness. After lording it over another cholesterol-rich breakfast at the South Bank, David Byrne strolled over to the Tower with some of the more provocatively clad members of the cast of *Ulysses in Nighttown* (which was playing at the Abbey Theatre that year). A visiting group of English journalists in Edwardian attire included Stan Gébler Davies, a copy of whose biography of Joyce in the museum library contained a warning note from Roland McHugh: 'This book is not recommended. Please do not display on shelves.' They were met by local traders Tom Fitzgerald and Peter Caviston (from the pub and restaurant of those respective names) with supplies of champagne and strawberries. The roof of the Tower was jammed for Barry McGovern's readings of the three short opening episodes of *Ulysses*, while for the benefit of those at ground level there were more readings outside by the Take 5 Theatre Company. Paul O'Hanrahan popped up in Fitzgerald's pub for a tabletop reading on behalf of the Balloonatics. Inspired by such activity, Dublin Tourism (as my employers were now named) were eager to promote and develop Bloomsday as a Dublin festival and used the occasion to stage a Bloomsday Garden Party in Merrion Square. There were Edwardian outfits, jazz music, wine and straw hats, and even a good quantity of accredited Joyceans, and while it may have had little to tell us about *Ulysses*, it served to bring together all the scattered pilgrims who had spent the day on the streets (and, it must be said, in the pubs.)

~ 1991 ~

Early in 1991, I applied for a new job.

Dublin Tourism had a new and major project in hand, supported by a truckload of money from the European Regional Development Fund to develop cultural tourism in Ireland. A magnificent house on Parnell Square was currently being restored and converted by them to house the Dublin Writers Museum. As the only curator of a literary museum already on the staff, I had inevitably watched the new development with interest and felt that it would be appropriate to widen my horizons. I duly applied and was appointed as Curator of the Dublin Writers Museum, but the museum was still a building site and I continued working at the Tower until things were more advanced.

Meanwhile, money had also become available for works to be carried out at the James Joyce Museum, and I learned that there were plans to transfer the collection to the Dublin Writers Museum to fill up its empty rooms and restore the Tower to the way it had been in Joyce's time, perhaps using it as some sort of catering venue (the words 'Bloomsday breakfasts' were used). The situation taxed my discretion, and having first advised that the transfer should be by way of a loan, I also proposed that as our many donors had given their treasures to the James Joyce Museum out of respect for its location, we should write asking their consent to move them.

This did not endear me to the management, but letters were sent, and while, to my chagrin, some of the donors obligingly gave their consent, others were not so pleased and word got out to the media.

My assistant, Ciaran Taylor, was appointed Acting Curator for the season in my place and started at the beginning of May. I had first met him on Bloomsday 1982 when I was representing the Reverend Hugh C. Love and he was portraying J.J. O'Molloy, and he had worked with me for the past few years. Ciaran was a mathematician and an artist, and a more orderly and methodical person than myself. Our first task was to order a skip and fill it with broken furniture, pieces of board, old posters and other junk which had accumulated in the building. Ciaran set up systems for daily records and stock control and later made up a template for a collection register.

*A Personal History of the Joyce Tower and Museum*

Roddy Doyle's book *The Snapper* was launched at the Tower in June.

On Bloomsday, in a departure from custom, it rained. We entertained the usual host of press and photographers, and after an interlude with the Balloonatics, Conor Farrington performed readings from *Ulysses*. As Ciaran was now officially in charge, I hitched a ride in a horse-drawn cab and went on into Dublin for the various festivities which normally I would not get to see, including a street party in Eccles Street to which I had given some help. Bertie Ahern, Minister for Labour at the time, unveiled a plaque at the door of the Mater Private Hospital on the site of No. 7, and the Diceman was present dressed up as the front door of Bloom's house (I had given directions for the wording on the letters attached to the doormat at the back of the costume). Harrison's Restaurant had opened on the site of the original establishment, and I dined there with the James Joyce Institute before attending a repeat of the Garden Party in Merrion Square. Here I was roped in by Ken Monaghan as one of his fellow-judges in the *Ulysses* Character Lookalike Competition. Among several Bella Cohens (who tried to bribe us with 'special rates'), Gertie MacDowells, Leopold Blooms and James Joyces (as well as Philip Mullen as Garryowen), we awarded the prize to a consummate Father Conmee.

Among the last evening events at the Joyce Tower were a lecture by Vivien Igoe in June 1991 on James Joyce's Dublin residences and a performance of 'Ivy Day in the Committee Room' in October to mark the centenary of Parnell's death. The planned transformation of the round room meant that it was no longer to be used as a space for lectures and performances, and the forty or so stacking chairs that had cluttered it up could now be removed. While the events had continued, we had been obliged to charge for them and they rarely pulled in sufficient audience members to cover the cost of putting them on.

In July 1991 I began working full-time with the rest of the team to set up the Dublin Writers Museum. Pat Seager, the director, made the reasonable and practical decision that there was no need to take the collection from the James Joyce Museum and settled for just two items – the large portrait by Basil Blackshaw and Joyce's piano, both of which would be better displayed and preserved in the house in Parnell Square. Over the next few months we worked hard to assemble and register the collection, organise display cases and write texts for labels and information panels. We had upstairs offices, computers and printers, archival storage and conservation materials, and a rambling building to work in. On the night before we opened in October, I was on my back under the display cases putting in screws until 4 a.m. The day of the official opening in November was confirmed only after I had accepted an invitation to give a lecture on Joyce in Syracuse in Sicily. I flew back to Dublin on the day of the opening, prepared to come straight from the airport, but my baggage had gone astray and by the time I had gone home for a suit, the speeches were over.

~ 1992 ~

With the Dublin Writers Museum open, it was the turn of the James Joyce Museum to get some attention.

## *A Personal History of the Joyce Tower and Museum*

In the week before Christmas, we had been busy packing up the contents, which were taken into storage in the New Year while work began. The walls of the Tower were stripped down, sandblasted and repointed. The round room and magazine were repainted, but the stairway was left with the original bare stone walls. The single staff toilet was replaced by two separate ones. The troublesome back window was timbered in and a blind fitted to the back door to reduce the light levels. The bucket-shaped lamps were replaced with track lighting, and extra lights and a secure handrail were installed in the stairwell. The lead flashing around the extension roof was entirely replaced and signage was added at the front. The gravel forecourt, a perpetual source of ammunition for small boys, was replaced with a granite patio, the ground at the side was landscaped and planted, and floodlights were installed to illuminate the building after dark. The display cases were relined and repainted in a gentle shade of grey which complemented the stone walls and highlighted the exhibits. To end the tiresome business of banging nails into the walls (particularly the granite ones), I specifically asked for gallery rail, which was fitted along the tops of all the walls and facilitated the hanging and moving of all pictures in whatever place was required.

The building work was complete by the end of April 1992 and I came round with a couple of colleagues from the Dublin Writers Museum to put the collection back in place and dress the round room. The café plan had mercifully been scrapped at a late stage, but it had been decided to go ahead with the restoration of the round room to the way it had been at the time of Joyce's stay and as described in *Ulysses*. I was asked to come up with the specifications and got most of my information from Gogarty's description of the room in *It Isn't This Time of Year At All!* in which he mentioned the shelf which ran around the room, piled high with tinware, and the positioning of Joyce's bed 'where the figure two is on a watch dial' (unfortunately, Gogarty failed to say whether the figure twelve was at one of the doors or at the fireplace — so I took the most likely option and located the bed in the north-east corner). It seemed appropriate to place the table in the centre of the room like the altar in a church, and to have trunks and suitcases as referred to in *Ulysses*. In an odd aberration, Joyce described the floor as 'flagged', which I decided to ignore, and I also pointed out that, although he gives Haines a hammock in the book, there was nothing to sling it from; the builders, however, had no qualms about drilling a couple of steel hooks into the walls for this purpose. The inventory in Gogarty's lease referred to a range, and a small but heavy iron cooking range was sourced and brought up with considerable effort through the old doorway to be installed next to the fireplace. Pots and pans, teacups and plates, beer bottles and books and various items of clothing were put in for effect. Wary lest the whole project be taken too solemnly, I finally added the black panther to the scene, snarling in the fireplace as an embodiment of Trench's nightmare. The overall effect was of a stage set rather than a total reconstruction, and the side of the room next to the staircase was left clear, with a couple of text panels on the walls.

After the experience of setting up the Dublin Writers Museum exhibits, I took an entirely fresh look at the James Joyce Museum, which in recent years had come to resemble the 'Haunted Inkbottle' even more closely. I removed numerous objects from the cases dating from after Joyce's lifetime and which bore witness not to his life but to his posthumous reputation – centenary medallions, articles and documents signed or given by people who had known him. The material in the entrance hall was arranged chronologically to follow Joyce's working life in Dublin, Trieste, Zurich and Paris, with the first edition of *Ulysses* occupying a central position opposite the entrance into the Tower.

In the more intimate surroundings of the gunpowder magazine, the more personal aspects of Joyce were now to be found – his death mask, his letters to Paul Ruggiero, his trunk, waistcoat, tie and guitar – and relics of the Dublin people, places and products that he had immortalised in his works. I reduced the number of photographs on the walls to a select few, restricted the portraits of Joyce to those that really seemed to matter and which were not based on already well-known images, and gave preference among the other paintings to those that were in some way informative. The motley accumulation of labels, typed or printed in different fonts and sizes, were replaced with uniform captions in the same style. Bono strolled in while we were at work and gave us his blessing. The job was finished off with a new entrance desk equipped with a counter, drawers and cupboards, and space to keep reference books and office work out of sight of the visitors. With room behind the desk for more than one staff member, the office space at the back of the room was done away with and the photocopier removed. Bookshelves were put up for the display of sale stock.

Back in the Dublin Writers Museum, there was still no escape from Joyce, whose work had gone temporarily into the public domain fifty years after his death. (A European Union ruling extending this to seventy years was introduced shortly afterwards and enabled Stephen Joyce to rule the Joyce estate with an iron hand until the end of 2011.) The papers that Paul Léon had saved from Joyce's flat in wartime Paris and entrusted to the National Library of Ireland were unveiled in April 1992. Thanks to having met Alex Léon in Paris in 1980 and having kept in contact with him, I was able to put the library in touch with him for the occasion, which also included an appearance and a characteristic speech by Stephen Joyce.

The James Joyce Symposium was returning to Dublin and I was back on the organising committee. Some of the sessions took place in the Dublin Writers Museum, and I put together an exhibition of the photos of *Ulysses* characters which I had collected so far. On Bloomsday I was free to be a pilgrim, and went from an early breakfast at the South Bank to a later one at the Joyce Centre and on to attend the keynote symposium lecture in Trinity College, given by John Kidd. I remembered Kidd from his visit to the Tower ten years previously. On that occasion he had startled me by his devotion to numerology and his claim that Joyce had deliberately arranged every instance of the word 'yes' in the 'Penelope' episode on the pages of the first edition to form a meaningful pattern. In the intervening years he had become famous as an outspoken critic of the new *Corrected Text of Ulysses*, attacking its editorial practices and identifying some of its more dubious readings. Backed by Boston University, he announced that he would produce a superior and definitive edition. Expecting great things, the Joycean elite hung upon his lips as David Norris in full Bloomsday regalia performed the introduction. The lecture, however, felt derivative and obscure. After about five minutes, ashen-faced Joyceans began to slip out of the auditorium to enjoy Bloomsday elsewhere. David Norris remained on the stage, turned to stone behind his sunglasses, and Fritz Senn stayed to the end to see how many people would be left. I survived about twenty minutes. Later in the week I participated in a workshop to talk about the research and thinking involved in the recent reconstruction of the round room in the Tower.

Despite the excitement, variety and constant activity of working there, the Dublin Writers Museum was failing to meet the ambitious financial expectations of Dublin Tourism, and economic measures began to eat into the staffing budget. Later in the summer I was shocked to be told I was being moved back to my previous position as Curator of the James Joyce Museum, and over the next year the rest of the original creative team that had set up the Dublin Writers Museum was gradually purged and replaced by a new and lower-paid administrative structure. When I returned to Sandycove in September, Ciaran Taylor was somewhat nonplussed to revert to his assistant role after his season among the refurbishments. I spent the winter recovering from this change in fortune and putting in order all the paperwork belonging to the museum, including the files in the office in Dún Laoghaire which were to be transferred to the Tower. During the off season I was also occasionally 'lent' to the Dublin Writers Museum, which was finding it hard to get by without a curator.

Up to now, life in the Joyce Museum had been fairly free and easy and I had been allowed considerable latitude to get out, make contacts and contribute to the growth of Joycean activity at all levels throughout Dublin and beyond, raising the profile of the museum as part of the Irish cultural scene. The new emphasis in Dublin Tourism was on the commercial imperative, on company loyalty and business management. For the moment my inclination was to keep my head down and devote myself to the museum and its care and wellbeing, and to justify its existence and mine by keeping costs down and turnover high. The succeeding years, though not as varied as before, would have their moments.

## ~ 1993–6 ~

Someone else who was keeping his head down was Salman Rushdie, who had been put under fatwa after the publication of his novel *The Satanic Verses* and subsequent outrage among religious fundamentalists.

After a year or so in hiding, dodging death threats and assassins, he had agreed to attend the 'Let in the Light' conference in Trinity College in January 1993 and travelled to Dublin in secret, where I was asked to arrange a discreet visit for him to the James Joyce Museum. No doubt the cannon-proof walls provided a welcome sense of security. The conference was the first of his public appearances since the fatwa was imposed, and, as the years went by, he became a prominent advocate for the right of authors to express their opinions.

From the files I moved on to the compilation of a proper handwritten register of the collection similar to the one I had created in the Dublin Writers Museum. Previous such records consisted of periodic inventories which were updated, rewritten and retyped every few years, dating from the transfer of the museum to the tourism organisation in 1964 when all the items were listed according to location. Ciaran had made a start on this but I began afresh, giving every object an index number and a detailed description; recording all we knew about its provenance and date of acquisition; listing the related documents on file; noting its location in the museum and also reserving a space for miscellaneous comments, for instance relevant references in *Ulysses* or Ellmann's biography, or what Richard Hamilton said when I showed him some artwork wrongly attributed to him. The work drew me into a closer and more intimate relationship with the collection and reconciled me to staying with the Tower.

When Dublin Tourism moved out of its head office in 1995 and set up quarters in St Andrew's Church in the city centre, I was left at a peaceful remove, working away in the museum. Under a new administrative structure, the company's visitor attractions – the Tower, the Dublin Writers Museum, the George Bernard Shaw birthplace, Malahide Castle and the Fry Model Railway – were put under a single manager and marketed together as Dublin Tourism Enterprises. New incentives, such as a combined ticket arrangement and printed visitor leaflets, were introduced, and increased emphasis was put on sales. One of the fortunate results was that I was able to point to increased visitor numbers and make the case for extending the season to seven months, from the beginning of April to the end of October. For the winter, however, I was expected to work at the Dublin

Writers Museum. My reinvolvement in duties there meant that there was less time to work on off-season projects and look after visitors to the Tower.

As Joyce memorabilia continued to fetch high prices in the marketplace, the museum collection, which relied mainly on the kindness of donors, was no longer expanding at the same rate and the material that came in was more related to the Joycean background. I was still pleased to receive an original watercolour of the Tower, clearly dated 1904 and showing the ladder below the front door. Another informative artwork was presented by designer and film art director Tony Inglis, who in 1954 had painted the scene from 'Nausicaa' based on his own memory of the beach below Leahy's Terrace before Beach Road was built and the shore reclaimed. Something more directly connected to Joyce, however, was a pair of prints by Stella Steyn, an Irish-Jewish artist who was introduced to the Joyces in Paris and became a friend to Lucia. At Joyce's invitation, she made some drawings illustrating *Work in Progress* to appear in the literary journal *transition*. Two of the prints featured in a retrospective exhibition at the Gorry Gallery on Molesworth Place in 1995 and were donated to the museum at the request of her family.

Bloomsday had taken on its own momentum, and the annual hordes of pilgrims no longer needed reminding that the museum would be open from 8 a.m. and that visitors were welcome to do their own readings and strut their Bloomsday stuff. The desk staff were kept busy with the office rubber date stamp, which I had recently upgraded to include a picture of the Tower and which became a desirable addition to postcards and copies of *Ulysses* (some of which accumulated stamps from year to year like well-travelled passports). Other local restaurants, pubs and traders had followed the lead of the South Bank in serving up Bloomsday breakfasts, bringing in musicians, pouring pints and turning the day into a gaudy garden party. The task which I had assigned myself over the past dozen years of Bloomsdays – to collate and issue a programme of all the planned Dublin celebrations – was now a monstrous one running to several pages, made at least more merciful by access to a vintage word-processor (which, like the typewriter before it, had problems printing the letter 'a').

The Diddlem Club brought its own re-enactment of 'Telemachus' to the Tower in 1995, with Haines represented as Britain's Prince Charles and gratuitous passages from 'Cyclops' inserted into the action.

In 1996 Barry McGovern, who had been unavailable for a few years, returned to the Bloomsday slot, which became a regular annual fixture for him and an appropriate public homage to Joyce's great novel. This was also the year when the James Joyce Centre was finally opened to the public after years of fundraising, restoration and preparation. It would go on to become a major player in Bloomsday celebrations – and a competitor with the Tower and Sandycove and Glasthule for press coverage on the day.

The museum had never had a letterbox, and although post could be shoved in underneath the front shutter, I made an effort to be there in the mornings before the postman came on his rounds. I could always, however, rely on Denis Burton, Sandycove's favourite deliverer, who knew that he could usually find me taking my morning swim at the Forty Foot at the same time as his own dip. The author of an article in the *Sunday Independent* in 1996 was surprised to witness Denis arriving at the bathing place with a handful of envelopes and a package to give to a swimmer who emerged from the waves to accept it. Denis, who died of cancer not long afterwards, is commemorated with a seat in the nearby Otranto Park.

Václav Havel, Czech president, playwright and hero of the Velvet Revolution, visited the museum later in June 1996, during his state visit to Ireland. I was on holiday in Gorey at the time and drove up to Sandycove to meet him.

One of the first visitors of 1997 was Ewan McGregor, who came in with Pat Murphy, director of the film *Nora*, in which Ewan would portray James Joyce. I supplied him with a copy of the recording of Joyce's reading from *Anna Livia Plurabelle* to help with his preparations. In an unusual catering exercise in May, RTÉ took over the Tower for a day to entertain the Eurovision heads of delegations to lunch, although we did not get any of the performers. On Bloomsday we had performances by Paul O'Hanrahan and the Diddlem Club, but I saw little of them as I was busy downstairs with a young fellow named Ryan Tubridy who was reporting for *Today with Pat Kenny* on RTÉ radio. The radio link was giving trouble and, in the end, we had to do all the interviews by phone.

~ 1998–9 ~

In 1998 Bloomsday happened twice, the second time being in July at the behest of the Bord Fáilte photographic section, who had somehow failed to get coverage of the actual day.

## A Personal History of the Joyce Tower and Museum

They asked me to round up a band of actors and Bloomsday regulars to adorn the premises in their Joycean outfits. They included the Dublin gallery owner Gerald Davis, well known as a Leopold Bloom impersonator since 1977 when he noted that he was the same age as Bloom, a Dublin Jew similar in appearance to Joyce's description of him, and having more than 'a touch of the artist' about him; Bloomsday perennial Nora Connolly; former Miss Ireland Nuala Holloway, who had given a couple of racy readings of 'Penelope' on previous Bloomsdays; and Wildean David Rose, who brought a touch of the Naughty Nineties to the proceedings. The weather, however, arrived before the photographers did and the shoot remained unshot.

Books continued to accumulate in the museum library. Visiting scholars and translators were generous with copies of their works, and if I could not obtain a new book by gift, I could order it from our book supplier for sale and take a copy out of stock for the library. The bookcase which I had once considered capacious was quite full and I had been forced to make room by storing some of its contents in boxes and moving the more frequently used reference books to the reception desk. Any book which could be considered a 'museum object' – for instance, the first editions of Joyce's works which were on display – was registered and kept separately. This category did not expand quite so quickly and a couple of years separated the presentation in 1997 of the 1926 Odyssey Press edition of *Ulysses* and the gift in 1999 of the first Japanese translation of *Ulysses*, published in 1931 and notorious at the time for having been produced without Joyce's permission or any payment to him.

Since 1987 it had been the practice of the James Joyce Institute of Ireland to conduct a 'pre-Bloomsday walk' following a part of the action of *Ulysses* on location with ad hoc dramatisations and readings. The annual walks so far had covered most of the city centre episodes, but in 1999 the Institute took itself to Sandycove to re-enact 'Telemachus' in some detail at the Tower, attempting to establish the precise location of each line. The rooftop section had, of course, been done to death over successive Bloomsdays, but the conversation in the round room and on the path outside was less familiar territory. For final authenticity I was obliged to shed my garments at the Forty Foot and plunge into the sea while uttering the words of Buck Mulligan: 'He who stealeth from the poor lendeth to the Lord. Thus spake Zarathustra.'

After twenty years of Bloomsday at the museum, it had become something of a routine, if no less busy or enjoyable. In the days leading up to 16 June, I would be constantly updating the 'Bloomsday in Dublin' events sheet (which now covered a whole week of activity), taking calls and visits from journalists, attending Joycean events if I had time, laying in extra stocks of *Ulysses* and other items for sale, and leaving the building ready for action the night before. The South Bank had changed hands and no one was any longer doing breakfast at seven o'clock, so I would eat at home and cycle to Sandycove in time for an early morning dip at the Forty Foot (occasionally attended by other Bloomsday celebrants or roving journalists) and the donning of my Bloomsday finery. As Buck Mulligan remarks, 'we'll simply have to dress the character'. I had given up the cliché stripy blazer and straw boater and now wore a white cotton suit, a vintage white waistcoat and a brightly coloured tie, accessorising with a fob watch (stopped at 4.30) and chain and a pair of cufflinks made out of Victorian silver threepenny bits. Anyone waiting outside the museum before eight would have to wait while I went inside to open the shutters, turn on the lights and raise the flag.

The first people through the door would usually be hardy annuals with their own routine of having their copy of *Ulysses* date-stamped, writing their names in the visitors' book and going up to the roof to start reading aloud (with the emphasis more often on delivery than on performance). The payment of admission fees was part of the ritual and was an occasion for me to engage personally with each visitor as they came in. Des Gunning and Tina Robinson were regular first-footers, and Jim Carroll and his wife Breda would arrive with their friends by horse and carriage. Most outfits were inspired by notions of Edwardian costume, but there were occasional evocations of the master himself with hats, glasses and canes, and now and again something truly imaginative, such as the eight people who arrived in T-shirts individually printed with the names of the male yellow and white children to whom Leopold Bloom gives birth in 'Circe' – Nasodoro, Goldfinger, Chrysostomos, Maindorée, Silversmile, Silberselber, Vifargent and Panargyros.

For the long and busy day that was in it, I would have two assistants on a staggered roster so that one would come in at nine o'clock and the other at ten as the day got steadily busier. As soon as I could get away from the desk, I would check out what was happening upstairs, talk to journalists and be ready to meet Barry McGovern when he arrived. His first reading would begin around 9.30 a.m. and I would need to interrupt the other readers as diplomatically as possible before launching him on his way. Barry would position himself next to the pole in the middle of the gunrest and move slowly around it while reading so that he would face everyone arranged around him as he proceeded. I would slip downstairs from time to time to attend to other duties or to allow one of the assistants to take in part of the performance. Between the readings (which lasted about twenty-five minutes) there would be a break which allowed one audience to disperse, if they wished, and another to gather.

By the time the second reading began, the building would be crowded with people and would usually remain so for the rest of the morning. To get up or down the stairs, it was necessary to wait until there was no one approaching in the opposite direction and to make a dash for it as soon as the opportunity arose (Barry remarked on more than one occasion that I should install traffic lights for the day). Unbooked groups put particular pressure on the arrangements. The top of the tower was a seething mass of Joycean humanity, while down at ground level it was normal to find other (unscheduled) events going on outside on the patio.

Peter Donnelly, a ribald rhymester known as 'The Racker', would usually pop up in the late morning with a performance of his 'Bloomsday Rack', and Barry and I would escape for a lunch break in the no less quiet surroundings of Fitzgerald's once the crowd had peaked. As he tackled longer episodes of *Ulysses*, Barry's readings often continued into the early afternoon, but the crowds would dwindle almost to normal levels after lunch and the serious Bloomsday celebrants would have headed for

A tie worn by James Joyce, presented by Samuel Beckett in 1979.

Robert Nicholson, curator of the James Joyce Museum, between Anthony Cronin (left) and Michael Scott at the reopening of the museum in 1979 (© Eastern Regional Tourism Organisation).

A first-edition copy of *Ulysses*, presented to the museum in 1980.

Three curators – Robert Nicholson, Vivien Igoe and Roland McHugh –
at the presentation of the first edition of *Ulysses* in May 1980
(© Eastern Regional Tourism Organisation).

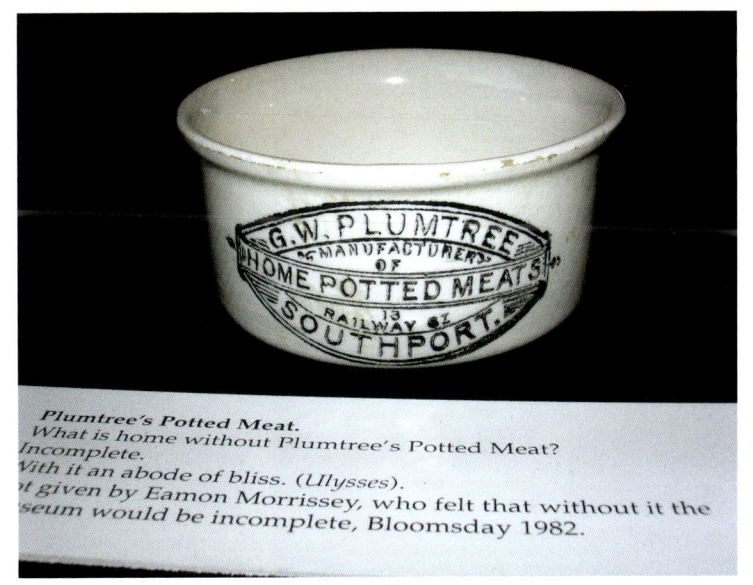

A Plumtree's Potted Meat pot, given by Eamon Morrissey on Bloomsday 1982.

Robert Nicholson and Clive Hart in costume for *O Rocks!* on Bloomsday 1982.

Brenda Maddox at the launch of her biography of Nora Barnacle Joyce at the Tower in June 1989.

Salman Rushdie (right) at the Tower in 1993.

Joseph Strick, director of the 1967 film of *Ulysses*, visiting the Tower in 2001 (© Godfrey Graham).

Senator David Norris being interviewed by telephone at the Tower on Bloomsday 2005.

Fritz Senn in the Zurich James Joyce Foundation, August 2007.

'Stately, plump Buck Mulligan came from the stairhead, bearing a bowl of lather on which a mirror and a razor lay crossed.' Paul O'Hanrahan performing at the Tower in August 2011.

Barry McGovern reading at the Tower on Bloomsday 2012.

Fran O'Rourke and John Feeley with James Joyce's guitar following its restoration in 2013 (© Mihai Cucu).

Minister for Tourism, Leo Varadkar, visiting the Joyce Tower on Bloomsday 2014, with Robert Nicholson and Vivien Igoe, representatives of Dún Laoghaire-Rathdown County Council and Fáilte Ireland, and members of the Friends of Joyce Tower Society (© Fáilte Ireland).

Ben Okri at the Joyce Tower in November 2015.

Bryan Murray reading at the Joyce Tower on Bloomsday 2017.

## *A Personal History of the Joyce Tower and Museum*

town or the local pubs. Inevitably after Barry had gone, someone would still be looking for readings and I would usually deliver one before disappearing in my turn around 4.30 p.m. to seek Bloomsday in town while the assistants kept the show going until six o'clock. I would be back in the morning to check the final figures and restore the museum to order.

The less glamorous side of the business was the maintenance of the building. The repointing carried out in 1992 had gradually deteriorated, and rainwater would work its way through the roof to emerge on the walls inside, or as drips and puddles in the round room. I installed a new dehumidifier and was kept busy with the mop. I had endless problems with the electric motor on the roller shutters and had frequent resort to the hand crank, which raised the shutter so slowly that the alarm was liable to go off before I had got sufficient clearance to dive under the shutter and get to the control panel. In 1998 the glass front door, which had steadily proved more and more difficult to open and was catching on the floor, collapsed when its hinges gave way (fortunately at a time when there were no visitors). The replacement door, apart from being six inches shorter, did not open any more easily and it was discovered that the steel frame around the front window area had become distorted.

Finally in 2000, a contractor was engaged to replace the frame and the entire front glazing. With a lot of pushing and shoving, I moved the reception desk, the cabinets, display stands and other furniture down the room and squeezed everything into the back two-thirds of the exhibition hall. The front was partitioned off for a few days while the contractors created noise and dust, and visitors were admitted through the back door. At the end of it, we had new windows in an aluminium frame, a new door, a new shutter and a new motor.

A somewhat different issue involved the flagpole on the roof, at which Sylvia Beach had performed the opening ceremony in 1962. Just after Bloomsday 1999, it was discovered that it was consumed with rust beneath its paint and was in danger of collapse. The men who came out to replace it began by tying a rope to each end of the new pole and trying to pull it all the way up the outside of the tower, but they were thwarted at every attempt when the pole snagged on the string course which encircled the wall a couple of metres below the top. After a lot of effort and head-scratching, we discovered that the solution was to lift the grating off the murder hole, pushing the pole at an angle up through the old front door into the machicolation above and thence to its place by the parapet.

~ 2000–2 ~

In June 2000 the museum received an out-of-the-ordinary presentation from Brendan Kilty, the Dublin barrister who had bought 15 Usher's Island, setting of 'The Dead'.

Brendan had also acquired the rubble of the demolished Joyce residence at 2 Millbourne Avenue, and arrived at the Tower bringing a large chunk of masonry with a strongman to carry it and a video crew to record the presentation, in the course of which he boldly referred to Number 15 as 'the most famous address in world literature'. To this I was bound to reply with an equal claim for the Tower. Brendan put another dozen years and a huge amount of work and money into restoring and opening 'The House of the Dead', but was eventually forced to sell it to a new owner, who only wanted to convert it into a hostel.

Visits by TV crews continued to be a regular feature. BBC came out to film the poet Tom Paulin at the Tower for their *Arena* programme in October that year, and two weeks later I obliged a Belgian travel programme by letting them film my morning dip in the Forty Foot. I was so cold afterwards that the interview about the museum had to wait until I had thawed out.

In February 2001 Channel 4 brought Joseph Strick to the museum to mark the release of his film of *Ulysses* on DVD and the final lifting of the Irish censor's ban on the film thirty-four years after it was made. Rosaleen Linehan, who had been in the original cast, also turned up for a morning of memories. In April the museum was the venue for a visit by the European Academy of Poetry, hosted by Michael D. Higgins, John F. Deane and Thomas Kinsella, and in May Canal+ came to interview me about John Huston's part in the founding of the museum for a documentary film.

John Huston was also in the news in July when his plaster copy of James Joyce's death mask was put on sale and was bought by the National Library of Ireland under the impression that it was an original. Colm Connolly in RTÉ came to investigate this and filmed an interview in the gunpowder magazine in which I had to reveal that the mask beside me was the original and that the one in the sale was a copy made from it by the Joyce Tower Society as a thank-you present for Huston after the opening of the museum. The library managed to get their money back.

The year 2001 saw the first performance by Paul O'Hanrahan of *Telemachus at the Tower*, a one-man site-specific rendition of the opening episode of *Ulysses* in which Paul did all the parts and stood in all the right spots, complete with yellow dressing gown, lather and razor and other appropriate props. He managed to continue talking in the round room while eating three breakfasts simultaneously and pouring milk. My role as keeper of the keys was to ensure that the heavy original door was unlocked and set ajar on cue so that light and bright air could enter. The performance continued on the path outside with a lively rendition of 'The Ballad of Joking Jesus' and down to the Forty Foot, where Paul was obliged for the sake of authenticity to remove his garments and plunge into the deep jelly of the water. *Telemachus at the Tower* was to become a regular event as part of the annual Heritage Week programme, with refinements worked in by Paul over the years. On rare occasions the car ferry even emerged from the harbour just as the mailboat in the text was doing the same thing.

In 2002 the National Library of Ireland made its most significant acquisition, of Joyce's notebooks and manuscript drafts for episodes of *Ulysses* which had turned up in Paul Léon's apartment. Michael Groden, who had assessed and authenticated all the material, was at the unveiling in the library and came to visit the Tower a few days later. The same week I had a visit from Nobel prize-winner for Physics Murray Gell-Mann, forever associated with Joyce for borrowing the word 'quark' from *Finnegans Wake* to describe a type of sub-protonic particle. He was accompanied by Leo Enright and a BBC crew. Further lustre was applied to the guest book the following week by Richard Hamilton, who was over in Dublin for his exhibition at the Irish Museum of Modern Art. Hamilton's drawings based on scenes from *Ulysses* were well known, and we had a rare copy of his poster for the Joyce exhibition at the ICA in London in 1950. Patricia Hutchins had given us some additional poster artwork for the same exhibition which she had claimed was also by Hamilton, so I produced it for his verification and when he denied all knowledge of it, I was at least able to set the record straight.

*The Ulysses Guide*, which had been out of print for a few years, was republished in a new revised edition in 2002 by New Island Books, and a launch party was held at the museum in June. Ken Monaghan did the official launching, and David Norris, Vivien Igoe, Peter Costello and other Joyceans were in attendance. On Bloomsday a visitor was observed reading *Ulysses* on a Palm Pilot, possibly the first use of a hand-held device other than a book for this purpose at this location. Unusually that day, not only did it rain but the building was practically empty at twelve o'clock owing to the Ireland-Spain World Cup football match, and when the Covenant Presbyterian Choir arrived to sing 'Love's Old Sweet Song' on the rooftop, they considerably outnumbered their audience.

In October Seán Walsh was making *Bloom*, his new film version of *Ulysses*. Unlike Joseph Strick, who had boldly updated the setting to the 1960s, Walsh was keeping it Edwardian, and the Martello tower used at the beginning was the one on Dalkey Island, without any modern clutter in the foreground. For the breakfast scene, however, the filming was done in the original setting in the round room of the Sandycove tower, with Hugh

O'Conor as Stephen Dedalus, Alvaro Lucchesi as Buck Mulligan and Mark Huberman as Haines. The furniture already in the room was used in the film, though the glass door to the staircase was temporarily removed and the frame disguised with a polystyrene surround. A few days later I spent a day on set in Dublin Castle as an extra and appeared momentarily in the final cut as the recipient of an improper letter from Bloom.

~ 2003 ~

In the build-up towards the Bloomsday centenary, the museum and its curator were constantly involved in 2003 as programmes, documentaries and projects were being prepared.

Seán Ó Mórdha, director of the acclaimed documentary in 1982, was making a new one, *Silence, Exile and Cunning*, focusing on what was happening in Joyce's own life in the key year of 1904, and came out to the Tower to discuss a structure. The film followed the progression of events from the opening of the year in the chaos of the Joyce family home and the writing of *Stephen Hero* to his move to Shelbourne Road, his meeting with Nora, the beginnings of *Dubliners*, the Feis Ceoil, the concert with John McCormack, the Tower episode and his departure into a new life of exile. Ó Mórdha used a team of narrators and commentators, including Vivien Igoe, Gerry O'Flaherty, P.J. Mathews, Luca Crispi, Katherine McSharry, John McCourt and myself. RTÉ radio brought Gerry O'Flaherty and Fritz Senn to the Tower to record the opening of their eighteen-part series *Reading Ulysses* in which they discussed each episode of the novel on location. Other film-makers included Charlotte Slovak, whose film

*Ulysse à Dublin* was made for French television, Fritzi Horstman with her documentary *Joyce to the World*, and Stacey Herbert and Patrick Martin filming *Following James Joyce ... from Dublin to Buffalo*.

Acquisitions also began to pick up again. Bookseller John Donohoe presented a large film poster for Strick's *Ulysses*, Eamon Morrissey came up with a bottle label from the Burton restaurant (where Bloom declined to have lunch), and with some available funding I was able to buy a 1936 first Bodley Head edition of *Ulysses* to add to the display.

~ 2004 ~

As we rolled into 2004, Roger Cummiskey presented a portrait of Leopold Bloom based on Joyce's own sketch of the character drawn in Myron Nutting's studio, and Tom Haran provided a bust of John Ryan, the modest secretary of the Joyce Tower Society who had ended up doing most of the work in the early years of the museum. Later in the year, Sotheby's auctioned a huge trove of Joyce memorabilia, mainly consisting of material that had remained in Stanislaus Joyce's possession in Trieste when James and his family left for Paris in 1919. Items such as Joyce's glasses, his Feis Ceoil medal and an original letter to Nora on Tower notepaper were beyond our slender means, but we managed to secure his Zurich ration book for the collection.

For the Bloomsday centenary year, the museum was open from the beginning of February to the end of October, justifying an early escape for me from the Dublin Writers Museum and a long and busy season with many requests for special tours, interviews, talks and articles. I wrote one history of the museum for the *James Joyce Quarterly* and another for a special Joyce issue of *Studies*, and put together an exhibition at the Dublin Writers Museum on Joyce's literary contemporaries in Dublin, tracing what they did during 1904 and where they were on Bloomsday. Oliver Gogarty, I discovered, was due to have returned from Oxford at the end of term but had lingered on for one final party (and might otherwise have come home in time to sweep Joyce off to the pub instead of his date with Nora).

I was running out of space in the Tower for any kind of a temporary exhibition but managed to borrow a display case and fill it with significant editions of *Ulysses*. Other larger exhibitions were on display elsewhere, including the National Library's impressive display of its Joyce holdings (augmented by rare material from the Buffalo collection) and the *Joyce in Art* exhibition at the RHA. Dublin's status as a centre of Joyce scholarship was recognised and enhanced by the arrival of established experts such as Sam Slote and Luca Crispi. The centenary provided an excuse to put up a few more Joyce-related plaques around the city, and Dublin Tourism asked me to select a few sites. We took the opportunity to mark the various houses where Joyce had lived or stayed during 1904 (although we decided it would be superfluous to put a plaque on the Tower). I also had one put up on the Loop Line bridge to mark the location of the cabman's shelter.

The James Joyce Estate were always stringent in all matters pertaining to copyright, and I feared the worst one day when Stephen Joyce rang up to talk about Barry McGovern's Bloomsday readings (which we had maintained was an ongoing performance begun when *Ulysses* was out of copyright and proceeding with

## A Personal History of the Joyce Tower and Museum

intervals ever since). Thankfully, he was in a good mood. 'I have no quarrel with you personally or with the Joyce Museum, at present,' he told me. 'You will do as you usually do at the Tower on 16 June.' However, he wanted to know 'why is everyone paying such attention to this centenary when the centenary of another Irish writer is being almost overlooked – Patrick Kavanagh ...?'

The James Joyce Symposium was back in town, and although I was on the committee, I found myself too busy that week to get to many of the academic sessions. I met many of the visiting scholars at possibly the most extraordinary of Bloomsday breakfasts, held on the Sunday morning in advance of the day. The whole of O'Connell Street had been roped off and occupied by crowds, circus entertainers and Joyce lookalikes, in the midst of which caterers were serving up rashers and sausages in paper bags for open-air consumption in an area filled with tables. While there was not even the smell of a kidney on the premises, this could be considered the ultimate homage to Leopold Bloom's solitary repast in the kitchen of 7 Eccles Street a hundred years earlier.

Bloomsday at the Tower was as mad as could have been expected. I was backed up by three assistants, one of whom was kept busy managing traffic on the stairs. A record number of visitors passed through the Tower throughout the day, and because they all paid in at the door there was a queue stretching across the patio outside. Barry McGovern started reading 'Cyclops' at 9 a.m., and took a long break in the middle of the day to go and meet Harold Pinter. In his absence, the museum hosted the première of Michael Holohan's musical piece 'The Snotgreen "C"', performed on the flute by Brian Dunning to great acclaim in the round room. The Racker presented his rack and David Norris called in later in the afternoon.

2004 marked another significant centenary, that of James Joyce's stay in the Tower in September. To commemorate the occasion, the James Joyce Institute visited the museum to read all the documents pertaining to that eventful week, including Gogarty's version of the episode and his letters to G.K.A. Bell at the time, Stanislaus Joyce's diary, William Bulfin's account of his visit to the Tower, James Joyce's letters to Nora from the Tower and the letter to James Starkey after his exit. For good measure, we also read some excerpts from *Ulysses*.

~ 2005–6 ~

Things steadily got back to normal after the centenary.

At a conference in Barcelona in May 2005 to talk about 'Putting *Ulysses* on the Map', I could not resist finishing with some personal experience:

> I should conclude by mentioning a recent incident which shows that there will always be fresh ways in which to encourage readers to explore Dublin through the pages of *Ulysses*. Earlier this month a visitor came into the bookshop in the James Joyce Museum, explaining that she was looking for a book, the title of which she had forgotten, but which she had heard could be followed through its settings in real places in Dublin. 'I read *The Da Vinci Code*,' she told me, 'so I want to read this one because it sounds very like it.' It was *Ulysses* that she was looking for.

## A Personal History of the Joyce Tower and Museum

Whatever about putting *Ulysses* on the map, I had for years been mentioning to the local authorities that there were no signposts anywhere pointing to Sandycove and not even a sign to show travellers when they had got there, so I was delighted when a 'Welcoming Stone' with a quotation from *Ulysses* on it was placed on the road near Fitzgerald's pub, and honoured to perform the unveiling in the week before Bloomsday.

In the midst of all this business, I had turned a blind eye to the pigeon's nest which had been constructed in the niche at the top of the stairs and the eggs that had been laid there. They duly hatched three days before Bloomsday and, while everyone was charmed by the chicks, it was the beginning of a nightmare that would go on for years. Pigeons took to roosting in the stairway, covering it in nesting material and layers of excrement, which I would have to wash out every morning. Elaborate netting systems were invented and put in place every night, usually to no avail, and I was driven demented by cooing noises at all hours of the day.

This was all still in front of me in June 2005. New Island held a star-studded book launch at the museum for *New Dubliners*, a book of short stories by contemporary Irish writers inspired by stories in Joyce's book. The next morning, Bloomsday began with a visit by David Norris, who took over the telephone to be interviewed by the journalist and broadcaster Eamon Dunphy and did another interview with TV3, who were waiting for him outside. Additional entertainment was provided by a group named Muldoon's Picnic, who gave a rousing rendition of 'Are You Washed in the Blood of the Lamb?' on the rooftop, before Barry arrived to read 'Nausicaa'.

July saw me in Washington to deliver a set of four lectures on different aspects of Joyce at the Smithsonian Institution, while in August I found myself required to spend three weeks at the Dublin Writers Museum covering for the manager in her absence. As the year drew on, the James Joyce Centre was obliged to close because of a lack of resources, and negotiations got under way. This resulted in it being reopened early in 2006 with government support and a reconstituted board in which I was retained as secretary with additional responsibilities.

Business continued as usual at the museum. I let visitors in and tried to keep the pigeons out, and when I had time to spare, I began the task of taking digital photographs of every item in the collection. I was finally able to buy a first edition of *Dubliners* to put on display, and at an auction later in the year I picked up a collection of photographs taken at the opening of the museum in 1962, along with a few related items. The two issues of *Time* magazine featuring Joyce on the front cover were kindly presented by Tom Reilly.

~ 2007–10 ~

As 2007 began, both the Joyce Museum and the Dublin Writers Museum were entered for the new Museum Standards Programme for Ireland (MSPI). This was an initiative by the Heritage Council to bring Irish museums up to a professional standard that would ensure the proper preservation of the national heritage and enable institutions to qualify for government grants and assistance. We were warned from the beginning that it would be hard work, particularly for small museums with limited resources. The early stages of application involved the filling in of detailed forms and the provision of extensive documentation establishing the status and ownership of museum buildings and collections. The hitherto somewhat ad hoc business of collection care and management had to be formalised and accompanied by policies, business plans and records. The Heritage Council provided useful training sessions in everything from label writing to disaster planning, and as the standard also called for suitable staff qualifications, I took a postgraduate diploma course in Museum Care and Management at the University of Ulster (my first experience of 'distance learning'), which began in October of that year. While we put a great deal of time and labour into the Museum Standards Programme, and it was of benefit, ultimately there were parts of the programme that were beyond the resources of the company, and after several years we would have to withdraw without achieving full accreditation.

Although it was not in the usual range of the collection, we were happy to accept the suit that Gerald Davis had worn over many years in the role of Leopold Bloom and which was given to the museum by his family after his death. Made to order by Louis Copeland, it was a replica of an Edwardian male mourning ensemble and would serve not only to commemorate Mr Davis but also to illustrate the physical reality of what Bloom wore throughout that hot day and where he stored the soap, potato, newspaper, watch, wallet and other contents. More directly connected to Joyce, however, was a first edition of *Chamber Music*, which we were able to acquire in the centenary year of its publication.

I spent an interesting couple of days filming a DVD named *James Joyce's Dublin: The Ulysses Tour* for Artsmagic. Loosely inspired by

*The Ulysses Guide*, it involved recording a brief introduction on location to each of the eighteen episodes. The director's plan was to film them in the order in which they appeared, but we soon abandoned this in favour of moving from one spot to the next most convenient. Having booked an early-morning filming slot in the Reading Room in the National Library, we had to contend with the sound of drills from a nearby building site, while traffic was a constant menace for the outdoor shots. However, the sun shone for us and we got everything done on schedule. I thought little more about it afterwards until I found museum visitors of all nationalities leaping on me with recognition.

On the strength of *The Ulysses Guide*, I had been invited to join an internet group named 'Ulysses for Experts', which lived up to its name by including such respected Joyceans as Fritz Senn, Clive Hart, Harald Beck, Vivien Igoe, Gerry O'Flaherty, Ian Gunn, John Simpson, Judith Harrington, Vincent Deane, Aida Yared, Sam Slote and John Gordon among its members. We applied ourselves busily to the minutiae of *Ulysses* and also to major matters like the timetabling of the book and mysteries such as what precisely happened on Bloom's train journey between 'Oxen of the Sun' and 'Nighttown'. In August 2007, several of us came together for a four-day workshop with Fritz at the Zurich James Joyce Foundation to discuss 'Cruxes in *Ulysses*' and to visit Joyce's grave and the local Joycean landmarks.

In between other activities, I was also commissioned to write a page on Joyce's Dublin for the updated new edition of *The Oxford Guide to Literary Britain and Ireland*, which appeared in 2008. It was a handsome volume and included (albeit buried away

*A Personal History of the Joyce Tower and Museum*

in the middle of the section on Scotland) a full-page colour photo purporting to show the Joyce Tower, but which to my horror was actually of the Martello Tower on Ireland's Eye and gave visitors the impression that they would have to climb up a rope to get in.

Scholarship, however, was little match for economics. The company now required me to spend a day at the Dublin Writers Museum each week during the season, and, to my further disappointment, the season was cut back in 2008 and the Tower closed for winter at the end of September. The recession became official later that year and the public service was put under a recruitment embargo, which steadily reduced the company's staffing levels.

My Damoclean situation reached a critical point in January 2009 when the administrator of the Dublin Writers Museum went on maternity leave and the decision was taken to close the Tower on Mondays and reduce my time there to two days a week during the season, with the other days covered by my two part-time seasonal assistants. The language schools which brought in many of our visitor groups also took a hit and our attendance figures dropped dramatically. September opening was cut out of the season before we even got there and I had to plead the case for group bookings in the off season. I did at least manage to open up for some special visitors in September at the request of Tim Carey, the Heritage Officer in Dún Laoghaire-Rathdown County Council, who had always been a supporter of the museum. His guests were the writers Paul Auster and Siri Hustvedt, who were in town for a book festival and particularly wished to visit the Tower. Siri was Norwegian, a pleasing coincidence because I was on the eve of departure to speak at a conference in Henrik Ibsen's birthplace at Skien with representatives of other literary heritage sites in Norway, the UK and elsewhere.

The Dublin Writers Museum administrator went to work in Malahide Castle when she returned from maternity leave and my situation remained unchanged. My postgraduate diploma was awarded in December 2009 but there was little opportunity to exercise my new qualifications. The Museum Standards Programme required a great deal of sustained effort, which my timetable could not accommodate, and most of my time was spent trying to stretch the roster to cover everyday business. There was some respite in April when my line manager called to tell me that she was moving office to the museum from Malahide Castle (where the former Dublin Writers Museum administrator was now in charge), and I would be able to spend three or four days a week at the Tower in summer. I was relieved. 'It certainly seems to indicate the power of prayer,' I told her. However, I was then required to cover the Dublin Writers Museum for the month of August while she was on leave, so my summer in Sandycove was a short one.

Bloomsday attracted the usual horde of TV crews, journalists and performers and also featured readings by Derry author Colm Herron from his new book, *Further Adventures of James Joyce*, a raunchy composition in which Joyce returns from the dead and spends twenty-four hours in Derry. With Bloomsday out of the way, I made some headway on the Museum Standards Programme and took a day trip to the Monaghan County Museum to see how things were done there. Among the directly useful exercises was the drafting of acquisition and disposal policies for the museum, which enabled us not only to say what kinds of things we wanted to collect, but also to decline politely when we were being pressed to accept material that told us nothing about Joyce or the Tower or which would be more appropriate to another collection. This was put to the test almost immediately when someone wanted to give us a framed photograph he had taken of Joyce's grave. We already had some pictures of the location on file and there was no need for us to take responsibility for accommodating another image of a monument erected after Joyce's death. The donor was disappointed but I felt it would be a waste of my work on the policy if I did not adhere to it.

~ 2011 ~

The year 2011 dawned with a whiff of doom about it.

Ireland had just been bailed out by the International Monetary Fund and stringent economic measures were in place. I had kept going through the past few years with the aid of two very dependable seasonal staff members named Catherine Murphy and Antoinette Morrow, but Catherine was due to retire in May and we would be unable to replace her. The pigeons had still not gone away, and since we were unable to take on a regular cleaner, this work also fell on the shoulders of myself and my assistants. As the day grew closer when most of Joyce's work would go out of copyright, the James Joyce Estate tightened its grip. I had prepared an updated edition of *The Ulysses Guide* for New Island Books, but instead of the steep but reasonable permission fee he had granted on the last occasion, Stephen Joyce now quoted a sum so prohibitive that we had to abandon the project. Barry McGovern advised not advertising that he would be reading

'Penelope' on Bloomsday in case the Estate decided to object to it being done by a male actor. News came in on the eve of Bloomsday that the Minister for Tourism and Culture would be visiting on the day, but he cancelled at the last minute and official recognition had to wait for another occasion. A well-informed Joycean told me at the time that the Department of Tourism was 'very keen on Joyce at the moment – you can expect a new James Joyce Museum to be set up in the city', which was good for Joyce but rather ominous for the existing museum.

Despite all the tension, Bloomsday was as pleasant as usual. *RTÉ News* filmed me devouring a packed Bloomsday breakfast, which had kindly been sent over by the Martello Restaurant (successor to the South Bank), and using the opportunity to deliver an impromptu lecture to a group of schoolchildren on the significance of the platter of offal. Stephen Joyce's more amiable cousin Bob arrived with his family, and Barry McGovern's performance of 'Penelope' was all that could be desired. Owing to rain, the final reading took place in the round room, which, in spite of the crowd, managed to convey most suitably the quiet and intimacy of the Blooms' bedchamber. This was also the Bloomsday on which I finally met The Order of the Finnegans, a select band of Barcelona writers obliged by the rules of their order to go every year to Dublin for Bloomsday and specifically to read extracts from *Ulysses* at the Tower before going for drinks at Finnegan's pub in Dalkey. They had usually arrived at Sandycove late in the day after I had gone and were well known to Antoinette, who did the late shift. One of them, Enrique Vila-Matas, had written a novel named *Dublinesque*, in which they appear.

## A Personal History of the Joyce Tower and Museum

In 2011 Dublin was proclaimed a UNESCO City of Literature, and a colourful book was published to mark the event. This time the photo of the Joyce Tower, though not as egregiously wrong as in the *Oxford Guide*, showed the Martello tower at Seapoint. Later in the season we had a visit from the BBC, who were filming an episode of the *Antiques Road Trip* in Sandycove and recorded an interview in the museum. The programme was still coming up in repeats a decade later. Another filming call brought me out before dawn for an art project by Fergal McCarthy, whose film *The Swimmer* was inspired by the 1968 Burt Lancaster movie of the same name. The opening shot showed Fergal standing perilously poised on the parapet before making his way round Dublin Bay in a series of swims.

In October I was approached by Professor Fran O'Rourke of UCD with a proposal to fund and carry out the restoration of James Joyce's guitar, which had been part of the collection ever since Vivien Igoe had brought it back from Zurich in 1966. Already well-worn before its arrival, it had been kept in various conditions over the years without the benefit of exercise and needed some work to repair damage and make it playable (which was also part of the proposal outlined by Fran as he envisaged some performances and recordings to recoup the cost of the restoration). He and his colleague, guitarist John Feeley, came to examine the instrument and we discovered an ancient plectrum inside.

~ 2012 ~

New Year's Day 2012 marked the date on which everything published by Joyce during his lifetime passed into the public domain and the control imposed by the Estate was finally lifted.

To celebrate the first day of copyright freedom, Paul O'Hanrahan came out to the museum to deliver a free reading of the opening episode of *Ulysses*. German students who were in the audience passed around whiskey and chocolate and a good time was had by all. On the same day Dublin Tourism was wound up and integrated with Fáilte Ireland, the National Tourism Development Authority, which was its original parent body. Fáilte Ireland's job was development. It existed on government funding and it did not have to rely on commercial activities to support itself. Though there were benefits to belonging to a much larger organisation – for example, it had a contract with a maintenance company which could attend to all our building, plumbing and electrical problems – Fáilte Ireland was not in the business of running museums and tourist attractions and had to adapt to its new acquisitions. For the moment, we put up new signage and continued as before.

At the beginning of March, I was informed that my line manager was being moved to a new position and that I was needed to be the administrator of the Dublin Writers Museum as well as its curator. The James Joyce Museum would no longer be open for regular hours, though group visits would be facilitated when possible, and the plan was to transfer its management to Dún Laoghaire-Rathdown County Council. Discussions had opened with the council and it was likely that the change of ownership would take place at the beginning of the following year. Bloomsday at least would be covered, but there were few consolations in sight, and shortly afterwards Owen Keegan and Tim Carey (the County Manager and the Heritage Officer) called in with the council architect to ask some preliminary questions and examine the premises.

Fran O'Rourke's proposal had been accepted, and I travelled with the guitar to the conservation laboratory in the National Museum of Ireland, where it would spend a couple of days in the hands of restorer Gary Southwell. RTÉ came in to film the work, which involved cleaning the guitar, repairing a crack in the wood, restoring some missing decoration, adding authentic strings and smoothing and polishing some areas roughened by use. The instrument was estimated to date from about 1820 and it was restored to the condition in which it might have been when Joyce was using it. The issue of making it playable was a somewhat contentious one, since it was a museum object and as such it should be handled as little as possible to ensure its preservation. However, to leave it mute was to deny it the opportunity to share with the present generation the same sounds that had come to the ears of its celebrated owner. Stringent conditions (no pun intended) were imposed to ensure that it would be handled only by professional museum staff and by a professional musician, specifically in this case the talented John Feeley, who accompanied Fran in all his concerts and who played the guitar for Bernadette Comerford of RTÉ Radio when she came to the Tower to record it.

While I still had the opportunity, I put up a notice at the Tower announcing that all future visits would be by appointment only. I put on my new Fáilte Ireland uniform and began trying to clear out as many old files as I could. It soon became difficult to facilitate every request for an appointment and I frequently found myself doing openings on my days off. I was reluctant to say that the museum was closed, in so far as it was still functioning, still had a curator, and was occasionally open to the public, and there were no plans to dismantle, sell off or remove the collection. However, ordinary members of the public tended not to see it that way, and any tourist using the previous year's guidebook was more than likely to be disappointed. Meetings continued with the council, who were committed to taking over the museum in 2013, and I entertained the hope that they might like to take me with it (if not as curator, at least as a consultant).

In a concession, and in view of the fact that the James Joyce Symposium had returned to Dublin, I was allowed to open the museum for most of the week of Bloomsday. I delivered the guitar to Newman House to be looked after by its amiable curator, Ruth Ferguson, in preparation for Fran and John's recitals there, and put in a busy week at Sandycove. I made one appearance at the symposium to speak on a panel with Gerry O'Flaherty and Terence Killeen on 'The Irish Reception of Joyce' and had to remain diplomatic when Gerry took the occasion to announce that the closure of the Tower was 'a disgrace'. On the way back to Sandycove I attended the final recital at Newman House and brought the guitar back to the museum for Bloomsday.

The day marked the fiftieth anniversary of the opening of the museum, but there seemed to be little to celebrate and we restricted ourselves to putting up a few balloons. As I opened the ceremonies at the top of the Tower, I announced that this would probably be my last Bloomsday as curator, little realising that it was only the first of several last Bloomsdays that still lay ahead. The day would have been more dismal had not Barry

*A Personal History of the Joyce Tower and Museum*

McGovern agreed to appear for an encore performance (or a *ricorso*, as he remarked) and gave an abridged reading of 'Cyclops' before disappearing at lunchtime. To fill the gap, I had to do some reading myself and Brenda Mc Sweeney came from Dalkey to give us a touch of Molly Bloom. The Tidy Towns Association hijacked the occasion by launching a local heritage trail on our doorstep, and we finished the day with a respectable 550 visitors.

In the week after Bloomsday, Fáilte Ireland was beset with outraged enquiries about the closing of the museum. Terence Killeen had an article about it in *The Irish Times*. Vivien Igoe echoed Gerry O'Flaherty's remark that it was 'a disgrace' and Joseph O'Connor and Declan Kiberd expressed their concern to me when they came to the museum for an RTÉ recording. I was also distracted by (unfounded) rumours that the Dublin Writers Museum was going to be closed, which would add further implications to my situation. Meanwhile a handsome new book called *The Martello Towers of Dublin* was launched by Dún Laoghaire-Rathdown County Council, which had not only got correct photos of all the towers but also included me in my Bloomsday suit in one of the pictures.

In July a meeting was held by the Dún Laoghaire Business Association to discuss a volunteer scheme to keep the museum open. I was unable to be present, but proposals were made in any case to support the museum by providing volunteers to keep it open whenever its owners did not have sufficient staff for the purpose. The proposals had originated with prominent journalist Vincent Browne, and Fáilte Ireland was inclined to accept the offer. A body named the Friends of Joyce Tower was set up to organise the volunteers and their activities. Since it would be a short-term arrangement until the expected takeover by the council at the end of the year, there would be no need for detailed terms and conditions, and although there would only be time to give minimal training to the dozens of voluntary assistants, I reckoned that the museum would survive the quiet end of the season. To save complications with cash handling and accounting, we suspended the admission fee and removed all the saleable stock. I had to remove or lock up all the confidential files, secure my computer and keep the phone line diverted to my office in the Dublin Writers Museum.

Arrangements were made with a security company to hold keys and come in at the beginning and end of each day to open and close the building, and because the daily routine of putting up and taking down the anti-pigeon netting was too complicated to explain to anybody, I warily dispensed with it. Some of the lingering maintenance jobs, like faulty lights and a sagging door, had to be dealt with before the volunteers arrived. By mid-August the scheme was set up and I met a group of thirty or forty volunteers at the Tower to give them a full-length guided tour and as much instruction as I hoped they would need, together with advice on the idiosyncrasies of the building and a request to interfere as little as possible with what they found there. I left some helpful reference books on the desk to assist with enquiries.

On 18 August 2012 the new arrangements were in place and the museum resumed daily opening. The volunteers each came in once a week to do a two-hour shift in pairs, so there were different faces throughout each day and from one day to the next, and I had to reinforce the need for communication and note-taking. They were generally very pleasant and friendly and enjoyed engaging with the visitors who came in, and although I occasionally had to ask them not to rearrange my desk or embark on unrequested DIY jobs, the scheme settled down quickly and the new arrivals made themselves comfortable. I called in occasionally to collect post, check the building and get feedback from the volunteers, and, until they built up their guiding skills, I continued to turn up to guide booked groups or to deal with special enquiries, for instance helping Shaun Davey to research letters from Nora Barnacle for a musical project he had in mind.

The local public started arriving in numbers once the word got around about free admission, a policy change for which the volunteers got the credit. The scheme was working well in terms of public access and satisfaction and it was decided to run it on into January, because the council had indicated that it wanted Fáilte Ireland to carry out some work on the building before it would take it over. I had to get in touch with various groups who had asked for tours in January and confirm that the museum would be open after all. With a continuing supply of willing volunteers, the society broke new ground by opening the museum for a few hours on Christmas Day and making themselves popular with the traditional Forty Foot plungers by serving mulled wine.

~ 2013 ~

As the New Year progressed, the volunteer scheme continued to be extended.

The architects who would be organising the works made their first visit in February, and when it appeared that it would not be possible to complete them before the season began, it was decided to start them in autumn. After nearly a year of working from one month to the next, this gave me a welcome further season as curator. The Friends of Joyce Tower had also begun to see themselves as more than a temporary solution, but a viable way of operating the museum in the long term. The prospect of a full season gave them the opportunity to establish themselves further through activities and through the raising of money from the donations frequently given by visitors in lieu of the admission charge. The money went towards printing information leaflets or other museum-related projects, such as a contribution towards the restoration of the guitar, which got another recital in February when Fran O'Rourke and John Feeley came out on a cold day to entertain a group of Fulbright scholars.

In April 2013 the Central Bank launched a €10 silver coin featuring a portrait of James Joyce, which got the seal of disapproval from his grandson. Whatever about the likeness, I noticed on closer examination that the extract from *Ulysses* they had used was misquoted. Terence Killeen had also spotted this, but the error soon created a demand for the coin as a collector's piece. Nonetheless, we decided not to include it in the museum. Something slightly more genuine was the new Dutch translation of *Ulysses* by Robbert-Jan Henkes and Erik Bindervoet, who arrived at the Tower to present it to the museum and read extracts on the rooftop. Other excitements included a reception for a group of delegates from the Department of Social Protection

## A Personal History of the Joyce Tower and Museum

and my continuing work, whenever I could get an hour or so at the museum, to complete a photographic record of the entire collection. The prospect of a change of ownership had made it important to distinguish anything that was being kept as a museum object from other bits and pieces which occupied the building, and I started going through the cupboards to identify books, photographs and other items that had accumulated there without going through the formalities of acquisition and registration.

Among the objects that I felt I had to keep was a pair of metal spectacle frames without lenses in a case with a cleaning cloth, which had been sent to me in 1991 with a letter from a woman in America, which read:

> Dear Sir or Madam,
>
> I am returning these glasses, which were left with me in 1971 or thereabouts. I was staying in London when a young man with whom I had a slight acquaintance visited me and left the glasses and glasses case which he claimed to be those of James Joyce. He said he took them when touring a place in Dublin that was a museum devoted to Joyce. I did not give it much thought at the time, but as he left and I subsequently did not see him again, the glasses ended up in my possession. I had a vague intention of returning them some day if it were convenient. I am sorry I did not make an effort to return them sooner.
>
> I want to clear my conscience in this matter, but discovered on looking in Fodor's Guide that there is not a single museum/birthplace devoted to James Joyce. Given

the limitations of my knowledge on where these glasses might have been kept in Dublin in 1971, I have decided yours is the most likely place. If not, I hope they will be restored to the proper owner.

Yours,
Virginia Parker

I knew that there had been only one James Joyce Museum in Dublin in 1971 and that there was no record of any spectacles having been in the collection. The thin wire frames were too light to have sustained Joyce's heavy lenses and were of a circular shape, which (contrary to popular opinion), he very rarely used. In addition, the case contained a glasses duster marked with the name of an optician in faraway Nainital, India, which was most unlikely to have been Joyce's. However, I had retained the parcel in the remote possibility that both the writer and her mysterious friend were telling the truth.

In early June we managed to arrange a series of evening recitals at the Tower by Fran O'Rourke and John Feeley. I had to be in attendance for each one to get the guitar in and out of the display case and to lock up the building at the end of the performance. John reserved Joyce's guitar for just one or two numbers during the recital and found that it required constant attention as the tuning pegs tended to slip. During most of the shows by Fran and John, I was downstairs minding the door and continuing the catalogue of the contents of the cupboards, but I was able to sit in on the special performance which included readings by Paul Muldoon. Among the audience were Seamus Heaney, his wife Marie and daughter Catherine, Paul Brady and Barry Devlin, and afterwards we adjourned to a local restaurant where I was presented with copies of the latest collections by Paul and Seamus, signed by all those present. It was a wonderful evening and we were all shocked by Seamus's untimely death a few weeks later.

As Bloomsday approached, I did an interview with Radio Perth in Australia in which listeners were led to believe that I was standing outside the museum in my Bloomsday suit instead of at the Vico Bathing Place with a towel after my morning swim. No longer fettered by copyright restrictions, the Joyce Centre had organised an ambitious project called Global Bloomsday in which sections of *Ulysses* were read and broadcast from cities around the world as the day progressed. Beginning in Melbourne and ending in San Francisco, the readings took place at local time and extended Bloomsday to about thirty-six hours. As a promotion for the event, the actor Frank Kelly (a Forty Foot regular) was filmed at the Tower and told me his memories of meeting Sylvia Beach there at the opening in 1962.

While I made the usual plans for Bloomsday, the volunteers independently organised a programme of celebrity readers to perform at the Tower on the same day, and we agreed that these should take place on the patio outside while other events took place on the rooftop, and the rooms in the museum were kept free for visitors to circulate. Without the formality of an admission fee, crowds milled in and out of the building and the extra volunteer staff were needed as traffic wardens on the stairs. At opening time, the amateurs began reading 'Telemachus' on top of the Tower, and when they got to the end of the episode, they started it again. At this point, I had to introduce Peter Gaynor, who was filling the spot previously occupied by the inimitable Barry McGovern and who also launched straight into 'Telemachus'. When I got downstairs to the patio, Pat Kenny was also reading 'Telemachus', and when Barry McGovern turned up with a group, he too read the same episode to them. After all this repetition, I was relieved when former actor Sabina Higgins, now wife of President of Ireland Michael D. Higgins, found something different to read and read it well. The day also included the presentation by Seán and Maebh O'Regan of a genuine old buttercooler (as referred to in the aforementioned 'Telemachus' episode) to add to the tableware in the round room.

As summer progressed and the Friends of Joyce Tower became further established, the realisation dawned that the arrangements made in the prospect of an imminent change of ownership had omitted to establish the appropriate parameters. As curator of the museum, I was responsible for its care, management and public representation and was also its spokesperson, and had understood that the volunteers were there to help keep it open with guidance and direction from me. The society, however, had a different understanding of their brief and believed they were there to run and publicise the museum and that my role was essentially to liaise between them and Fáilte Ireland and look after the collection. Fáilte Ireland did not seem able to clarify the situation, and I was already too busy at the Dublin Writers Museum to fight for my position. Moreover, the Friends were anxious to promote

*A Personal History of the Joyce Tower and Museum*

themselves to the future owners of the museum and to remain involved with it. My own intention was to do my duty by the museum and endure with some dignity until I could hand it over to the council representatives at the appropriate time, but the sheer protraction of the 'interim' period caused me great stress and uncertainty. I found the situation very hard to explain (especially in French) when I spoke at a conference in Nantes later in the year and was asked questions about the museum and how it was run. Although it was hard after all the years to find myself on the sidelines, the Friends were doing a great job looking after visitors, the volunteer scheme was recognised for what it had done for the local community, and the membership fielded an impressive array of talents and enthusiasm which were being put to the service of the museum. As time progressed, the Friends' committee would also play an important part in keeping negotiations with the council on track.

In October I regained some measure of possession when the museum closed for the promised refurbishments and I was given three weeks to throw out as much junk as I could and to sort and pack the collection, the library and all the other contents and furniture, to be moved and stored in a large unused exhibition room in the Dublin Writers Museum. The builders moved in when I had finished and the plan, as I told the society at its AGM, was to have the work finished and the museum ready to reopen in time for Joyce's birthday on 2 February. While the museum was closed, official announcements were made by UCD that the Aula Maxima (great hall) adjoining Newman House had now been designated as the location for what was described as 'a permanent museum devoted to Joyce's work and life', and I began to wonder whether my own life's work was due to be superseded. I was reassured by Éamonn Ceannt, chairman of the new museum, and Ruth Ferguson, the curator of Newman House, who asked me in for a meeting to explain the project and to make clear that it would not overlap with the role or activities of the Joyce Tower or the James Joyce Centre. The new museum would include other twentieth-century Irish writers but Joyce would be given special attention with a display of some of the items in the now vastly significant National Library collection. 'We're looking for a title without Joyce's name in it,' they told me. Ultimately, the title emerged as the Museum of Literature Ireland (MoLI).

~ 2014–15 ~

When we got into 2014, work at the Joyce Tower was running slow, and it became clear that the original deadline of 2 February would not be met.

The walls were surrounded by scaffolding and every inch of granite was being sandblasted and repointed in an attempt to weatherproof the structure. The pine floor in the round room was stripped back to its original colour, and all the paintwork was renewed. The ceiling in the extension had to be partly replaced and the flat roof re-leaded. New lighting was being installed throughout, along with a new electric switchboard and a set of heaters in the magazine and round room. The central pole on the rooftop, which had formerly supported a long-decayed weathervane, was replaced by a metal pillar. As the Dún Laoghaire-Rathdown heritage architect and I also discovered

## A Personal History of the Joyce Tower and Museum

to our dismay, the original front door had had its nineteenth-century metal plating (somewhat decayed, although still featuring its original studding), replaced with a plain steel sheet. Some final work was still going on at the end of March when I was allowed to regain access, and I was concerned to let the dust settle before I brought the collection back in. The volunteers were impatient to take possession and, under pressure, I was given little more than a fortnight to put everything into place although I had asked for a month. Apart from simply putting the entire display back where it had been, I also needed the opportunity to record all the material which was going back into storage and bring the location register up to date, so that if anything was being looked for it could be traced to the right box and the right cupboard. I had done a great deal of sorting while taking everything out, so although not everything was going back to the same place, it was now with other objects in the same category.

Among the improvements I had requested was the insertion of a vertical picture rack inside one of the cupboards so that pictures could be stored side by side instead of on top of one another. While the workers were still on site, they also attended to some minor jobs, such as freshening up the paintwork on the iron bedstead in the round room. The text panels that had been put in twenty years previously were renewed, and I also replaced some of the picture labels that had seen better days and made a new arrangement of the books in the library case. While money was flying around, I had the cracked glass replaced in a couple of pictures and got some minor repairs done. A portrait by John Butler Yeats of H.F. Norman – who, as the editor of

*The Irish Homestead*, had been the first to publish stories from *Dubliners* in 1904 – had been added to the collection and was put on display. Although there were still some works to be finished off, the museum was reopened at Easter and the volunteers re-established their presence.

The new developments provided a reason for the then Minister for Transport, Tourism and Sport, Leo Varadkar, to make an official visit on Bloomsday to reopen the museum and to pay tribute to the volunteers for their efforts. On the day he did not (to my disappointment) read Sir Leo's address to the ratepayers from the 'Circe' episode, nor (to my relief) did he wear a straw boater, despite my having been asked to have one ready for him. On his arrival, he was greeted by a welcoming crowd of council officials, Fáilte Ireland representatives and committee members and volunteers from the Friends of Joyce Tower (and also an individual in a boater and stripey blazer carrying a placard reading 'Fine Gael are shite and onions').

I brought the minister on a brief tour through the museum and up to the rooftop, where he made a speech and presented the chairperson of the society with a special Dublin edition of *Ulysses* which I had been able to acquire for the occasion. Refreshments in the round room were accompanied by a performance from Caitríona Ní Threasaigh, who was portraying Molly Bloom in a nightdress. As I noted in my diary, 'Mr Varadkar, who had never read his way to the end of *Ulysses*, arrived in the room to hear a stream of intimate female filth.' Our principal reader for the day was David O'Meara, who read all the way from 'Nestor' to 'Aeolus' at a cracking pace. After the minister had left, Richard

## A Personal History of the Joyce Tower and Museum

Boyd Barrett TD also came in to read the description of the municipal water system from 'Ithaca'.

Although the requested works had been carried out, the County Council did not yet move ahead with the takeover. Owen Keegan, who had originally backed the plan, had moved to Dublin City Council as City Manager. Another season had begun, Fáilte Ireland was covering all the costs of maintenance, insurance and curation, and the museum remained open and active thanks to the volunteers, so there was no urgency on them to take on a new responsibility. I had no idea how long I would remain as curator, what the future of the collection would be, or whether I could accept tour bookings more than six months ahead. The society now appeared fairly certain to be part of any arrangement under the council and were pushing for a controlling role when the time came. Meanwhile we were unable to proceed with the Museum Standards Programme because there was now no certainty about future ownership, staffing arrangements or collection care.

In September, the Culture Night programme was extended to the Dún Laoghaire area and the museum arranged a late-evening opening with tours by volunteers, several of whom had become proficient guides. I contributed my own tour, which, in a change from the standard one telling the history of the Tower and Joyce's stay there, concentrated exclusively on exciting items in the collection, an approach I felt obliged to describe as 'separating the room from the elephant'.

The renovations and repointing were no more successful than any of the previous attempts in keeping rainwater out of the building. I had long ago put cork studs on the backs of the pictures to prevent direct contact with wet walls, but the volunteers found the dampness alarming and I received concerned notes and phone calls from them whenever bad weather had its effect. The more vulnerable area was the round room, where the paintwork on the walls began once again to deteriorate, and there was the odd drip from the ceiling. The winter was enlivened by the Pat Kenny Christmas Day radio show, which was pre-recorded in the Tower in November. The researchers were impressed by the volunteers and recorded a tour given by their principal guide, James Holohan, and when they discovered that there was a curator of many years' standing, I was included in the programme along with the irrepressible Senator David Norris, Richard Boyd Barrett TD and author Martina Devlin (who was also one of the volunteers). Honor Heffernan and the Grafton Singers provided some seasonal music.

## ~ 2015–16 ~

The year 2015 was mainly marked by subterranean issues with the water supply.

Irish Water was trying to replace the worn-out network in Sandycove Point and there were weeks of cut-offs and pressure reductions. I shall draw a discreet veil over what was also happening with the sewage system but it ended with a directive that the museum toilets were to be reserved for staff use only.

Joyce's birthday was marked by a performance of Robert Gogan's popular show, *Strolling Through Ulysses*. There was also a proposal for a publicity stunt involving lighting up the outside of the Tower to resemble a huge birthday cake, which did not, however, go ahead. I continued to conduct the occasional guided tour at the museum and was glad to welcome Fritz Senn once again with a group from Zurich. The James Joyce Society of Sweden and Finland also made a repeat visit after many years, and Ferenc Takács, the Hungarian translator of Joyce, provided the same service for me when he brought a group of fellow Hungarians to the museum. Other visitors whom I met there were singer Edana Minghella and writer Ben Okri, who came out with a group from the British-American Partnership and read to them on the rooftop.

In June, New Island Books launched the latest edition of *The Ulysses Guide* (long-awaited after the fiasco in 2011). Several of the Tower volunteers were among those present at the Joyce Centre. Barry McGovern did the honours and we were also treated to a song by Andrew Basquille, a talented member of the Friends who could put a tune and a few words to any occasion. The search for a regular Bloomsday reader finally brought us to Bryan Murray, already well known to Irish audiences, who took up the narrative with 'Lestrygonians'. Caitríona Ní Threasaigh, who had brought Molly Bloom back to the Tower earlier in the week, gave a lively performance on the patio with Mary Pat Moloney as the washerwomen in *Finnegans Wake*, and other old friends were back to add to the day.

In July, I wore my curator hat to the commissioning ceremony of the LÉ [Línte Éireann] *James Joyce* offshore patrol vessel in Dún Laoghaire harbour, within sight of the Tower. The official naming was done by James Joyce's great-niece Carol Joyce, and others of the family were there for the occasion (with the usual exception of Stephen). Musical entertainment was provided by Darina

Gallagher and Sinéad Murphy, who had established themselves with their lively renditions of the many songs associated with Joyce's works.

The Friends had used some of their donation money the previous year to acquire a postcard sent by the Joyce family to the tenor John Sullivan, and now placed it on loan to the museum. The card was written by Nora and Lucia Joyce, while James, who was in Switzerland for an eye operation, could contribute only a shaky signature. It conveniently illustrated the Sullivan connection, as well as Joyce's medical history, and I added it to the display. Another addition to the collection, early in 2016, was a limited first edition copy of *Our Exagmination*, given by Malachy Prunty. Although I had to remove from display the existing copy, which had been signed by Samuel Beckett, the replacement was a rarer edition and in better condition.

As we moved into another year, the talks between Fáilte Ireland and Dún Laoghaire-Rathdown County Council continued without resolution, and I was concerned about the management of the collection and also that the museum would not be treated simply as a visitor attraction. From their now considerable funds the Friends added to the furnishings with some large blue executive chairs to replace the smaller, quieter, grey ones behind the desk, a display case for the book given by Mr Varadkar and their growing collection of well-deserved awards and trophies, a ponderous antique safe as a repository for donations, and a somewhat vulgar-looking picture of an Edwardian couple with the faces cut out so that people could pose in it for photographs. I had to request that the latter be placed at the far end of the patio so that it did not appear in pictures of the museum. A rather smaller and more acceptable item was a tin for Iron Jelloids kindly given to the collection by Séamus Cannon, illustrating the beneficial supplement which had done Gerty MacDowell 'a world of good'.

I continued to meet groups at the museum, including the bibliophiles of the Grolier Club of New York, the Dublin members of the International Women's Club, and representatives from UNESCO cities of literature from all over the world. In June, Fran O'Rourke and John Feeley arranged another series of evening guitar concerts in the round room. The British Ambassador, who was anxiously bracing himself for the Brexit referendum, had provided sponsorship for the event and treated the invited audience to a reception at his residence after the final performance, which had included contributions by Irish poets between the musical numbers.

Bloomsday featured a variety of performers and notable visitors. Bryan Murray was unavailable but he had kindly arranged for Owen Roe to fill in. While Owen was launching into 'Scylla and Charybdis' on the roof, downstairs visitors were being treated to the opening of a new operatic version of *Ulysses* by Eric Sweeney. The piece was only five minutes long and as RTÉ hadn't had time to get their cameras up, it was repeated before the cast moved off to Dalkey to perform the next number on location. The Order of the Finnegans turned up again from Barcelona and presented me with a printed programme, on the cover of which Cervantes appeared to be sitting on the rooftop of the Tower. Chanteuse Wendy Goodbody arrived with some musicians to entertain the visitors outside. Caitríona and Mary Pat reprised their performances of Molly Bloom and the Washerwomen. Cathaoirleach Cormac Devlin visited, sporting his chain of office. Phyllis Seigne, a redoubtable lady whose grandfather, Long John Clancy, had been portrayed in *Ulysses*, was present with her grandfather's walking stick. Ardal O'Hanlon, who was on a separate mission filming with Channel 4, appeared at the door and came in for a chat with Owen on one of his breaks from reading 'Wandering Rocks'. The next day Owen came back to pick up his bag and met a man outside who told him he was bound for the hottest pit of hell for what he had read on Bloomsday.

Meanwhile, the industrious Vivien Igoe had published her latest and largest book, *The Real People of Joyce's Ulysses*, a compendium of the biographical facts known about the numerous Dubliners and others who were name-checked in Joyce's masterwork. My own photographic project of many years previously had never gone particularly far and I was glad to pass on some of my finds to Vivien to add to her book. As I had some modest acquisition funds available to me, thanks to a kind donor, I used them to add the book to the Tower library.

As part of their negotiations with Fáilte Ireland, the County Council asked to do a valuation of the complete collection and needed access to all the cases and cupboards. We closed the museum for two days in November while their archivist came in to go through everything we had, from the items on display and in storage boxes, to the stored pictures, the portfolios full of unframed material, the library books and the photo files. In the course of the exploration, I came across more material that I had not had time to deal with in April 2014 and set about adding them to the register, which was now considerably larger than it had been four years earlier. We even discovered a couple of items that had been put on display at the time they had been donated and had somehow missed the formality of registration.

## ~ 2017–18 ~

The first gift of 2017 was for the museum library. Curiously titled *A Terrible Beauty: The Murder at Joyce's Tower*, it was presented by its co-author Michael Mahony (one half of the pen name 'V.M. Devine'). As the title suggested, it was a murder mystery set in the Tower, which in the story had been conveniently and temporarily cleared of its museum contents for a refurbishment job at the time of the crime. Another convenient stipulation of the plot was that there was an implausible private entrance to the building for the exclusive use of a neighbouring house on Sandycove Point. The book itself created its own mystery when it disappeared from the desk not long after I had registered it.

The storage boxes continued to yield up their supply of unregistered material for me to catalogue. As well as the spectacles of dubious provenance, I registered a collection of minutes and other documents from the meetings of the original James Joyce Tower Society, given by Con Leventhal's widow after his death, a 1903 copy of *The Irish Times* describing the royal visit, and the 1925 *Belvederian* with an obituary of George Dempsey, along with numerous other items of varying significance. Some of the books and publications already catalogued as part of the library were promoted to museum object status, including the issues of *transition* in which 'Work in Progress' had been serialised in the

1920s and 30s and one of the later Shakespeare and Company printings of *Ulysses*. As it appeared from the negotiations with the council, the ownership of the collection might end up in different hands from the management of the museum, and it was important to distinguish anything that should be preserved from other things in the building that ran the risk of being dismissed as old office contents and therefore disposed of.

My fortieth Bloomsday began as usual when I raised the flag at eight o'clock and said my short piece of welcome to the first arrivals, announcing (once again) that it was probably my last Bloomsday at the Tower but also that it was my fortieth as curator. We proceeded straight to the official first act of the day, a reading of the opening pages on location with Séamus Cannon as narrator, Andrew Basquille as Stephen and Aidan Coleman as a strangely mute Buck Mulligan in a yellow dressing gown and white shorts. Bryan Murray was back on duty reading 'Sirens', Wendy Goodbody and friends were back with more songs and music, and Caitríona Ní Threasaigh entertained as Molly. Even Cormac Devlin managed a return visit in his chain of office and Eamon Morrissey came in to be interviewed for a local video. In one of the madder manifestations of Bloomsday, I observed a group of Notre Dame University students going for a mass plunge at the Forty Foot, all in cheap straw boaters. Some interesting diversion was provided by a visitor who left in a copy of a photograph appearing to show James Joyce in a group with the Blackbirds dance troupe in Paris in 1929. I had to ask them for a better-quality picture before I could decide that the person in question might have won second prize in a James Joyce lookalike competition but was not the author himself.

*A Personal History of the Joyce Tower and Museum*

Storm Ophelia closed the museum for a day in October, but more serious disruption was caused by the combined forces of the weather systems known as The Beast From the East and Storm Emma, which brought three or four days of snow and wind at the beginning of March 2018, along with government advice to stay at home. Even when the museum reopened, the security company van was unable to drive out to open up in the morning and I had to come from closer at hand with my keys.

I continued to go through the collection with my camera and to update the registers. The negotiations with the council dragged on, delayed by some contention about who should own the collection. By this stage I was conscious that my own retirement was looming, and that, instead of walking the plank, I might perhaps find myself stepping on to the shore at the end of the journey.

On 1 May 2018 I reached a significant landmark as I celebrated forty years in office, and marked the occasion by conducting 'The Fortieth Anniversary Tour'. Momentarily thrown at the start by getting a speech from the Friends of Joyce Tower chairman and a song from Andrew Basquille, I led a group through the Tower for a talk based mainly on personal experiences. Most of those present were personal acquaintances who were already familiar with the history of the Tower, so I could concentrate more on the significance of the museum, the guiding principles of being the curator, and some of the many stories behind the objects in the collection. It was also a chance to pay tribute to some special figures along the way (including, for example, John Ryan, who was also remembered later that month with a plaque outside the Bailey restaurant).

The James Joyce Institute's pre-Bloomsday walk, which had been ringing all the changes since 1999, returned to 'Telemachus' on the sunny Sunday before Bloomsday and made another visit to the Tower, the Forty Foot and Dalkey Avenue. The museum was beginning a week of entertainments which would include performances from tenor Noel O'Grady and singing duo Darina Gallagher and Sinéad Murphy. On Bloomsday itself, I arrived to find two Portaloos parked directly beside the front door in anticipation of the day's demands, and paused only to quote, 'It is meet to be here. Let us construct a watercloset,' before opening up, raising a new flag and announcing (this time with total conviction) that this was my last Bloomsday as curator. Séamus Cannon and his colleagues repeated their performance of 'Telemachus' and Bryan Murray read 'Cyclops' in mixed weather in the round room and on the rooftop. Wendy Goodbody and her friends were back again, and the media were there to take pictures and do interviews.

Advised that the handover to the council could possibly take place in mid-August, I redoubled my efforts to update the registers. Every time I opened a storage box, I seemed to come across something else that merited being included in the collection, and there were also two new interesting acquisitions to record. Andrew Ward offered an excellent print of Berenice Abbott's famous portrait of Joyce from the original negative, which I was very pleased to accept. Important though the picture was, I was mainly familiar with the image from inferior reproductions and from countless dreary portraits of a constipated-looking Joyce that were inspired by it. There was nothing to compare to the sensitivity of the original image. Something less well known but no less desirable was an original manuscript verse by Oliver Gogarty, which was presented by Christine and Tim O'Neill and provided an excellent opportunity for a label reminding visitors of Gogarty's extraordinary career and character. Penned in one of his lighter moments, it reads:

*Said She*
'Never' said she, 'Pretend you care
For what I don or doff,
Because the better the clothes I wear
The more you want them off.'

Mid-August came and went, and I was told that the handover would take place on 31 October. I carried on putting the collection records in order and when I asked Fáilte Ireland how future acquisitions would be handled, they were somewhat surprised to learn that the collection was not 'finite' but still growing. For their further information, I supplemented the digital register with a scanned copy of the handwritten register which contained the fullest record of the collection. Some of the library books had been stored in the Dublin Writers Museum to make space and had to be returned. The filing cabinet and a number of boxes contained a whole new batch of uncatalogued material in the form of correspondence and archives, and the best I could do was to write summaries of the contents and advise Dún Laoghaire-Rathdown County Council of their importance.

When the handover was deferred again to 30 November, I decided that it was time for another tour on the 28th, styled 'The Farewell Tour'. Most of the people who turned up for this were the non-Joycean side of my acquaintance and I treated them to an in-depth history of the Tower. By the time it happened, however, the transfer date had been put off again and I turned my attention to a heating problem which was eliciting complaints from the shivering volunteers. Temporary heaters were delivered and early in the New Year the problem was solved and the museum had ceased to be chilly.

~ 2019 ~

At the beginning of 2019, I received notice that retirement from the public service at the age of sixty-five was no longer obligatory and I could if I wished work on for another five years.

I considered briefly whether I should dutifully hang on to see the handover through, and extended my working life by three weeks to give myself a final look through the filing cabinet and to be there for the next scheduled handover date at the end of March. After so many deferrals, however, I was not surprised when this too proved to be illusory due to a delay in the State Solicitor's Office.

Pleasingly, my final duties at the museum involved what I enjoyed most – letting people in and showing them around. I had to open the building at 6 a.m. on 26 March for a film crew to do their work, and on the following day I brought round a last group of American students before embarking on what was very definitely 'The Final Farewell Tour', an occasion as congenial as its predecessors and full of friendly faces. The next day I handed in my keys to Fáilte Ireland, said my farewells and embarked on my retirement.

I was relieved to have stayed long enough to put the collection in order, and to see some definite plans in place for the future of the museum and the appointment of a suitably qualified person to run it. I had been privileged to have been at the centre of the museum for so long, and although it now seemed to be heading in a new direction with the involvement of the volunteers, they had brought in a fresh wave of energy and expertise which would serve the museum well in years to come.

ROBERT NICHOLSON
September 2023

# THE FRIENDS OF JOYCE TOWER 2012–22

*Séamus Cannon, Director,*
*Joyce Tower and Museum*

UNDER ACUTE financial pressure, Fáilte Ireland, the Irish Tourist Board, closed the Tower in 2012.

This decision caused widespread upset within the local community and led to a demand for its reopening. There is unanimous agreement among those involved that well-known journalist Vincent Browne was the man who gave focus to the protest. Vincent approached Fáilte Ireland, who held the lease on the Tower, and Dún Laoghaire-Rathdown County Council. He gathered a small group of friends who each agreed to recruit others in sufficient numbers to staff the Tower on a volunteer basis. With enough volunteers, it would require only a small commitment of two hours a week from each to facilitate a seven-day opening.

A short while later a public meeting was held at which the Friends of Joyce Tower was formed. A committee was elected with Tom Fitzgerald as chairperson. The ambition was to keep the Tower open 365 days of the year, including Christmas Day and New Year's Day. Discussions were held with Bord Fáilte who directed the Friends of Joyce Tower to consult with the curator, Robert Nicholson. It was understood by Robert and by the Friends that this arrangement would be short-term only, possibly three months at most, until the lease was taken over by Dún Laoghaire-Rathdown County Council.

No one expected that the three months would last ten years, an odyssey for our times, mimicking that of Odysseus himself. During that time, the Friends of Joyce Tower changed from an ad hoc grouping into a significant cultural and community organisation which has brought Joyce to the people in a unique way. Staffing the Tower remained the primary role of the volunteers. Bord Fáilte, as managers of the property, were helpful and cooperative throughout this period and at one point undertook significant restoration work in the endless battle against the weather.

Negotiations with Dún Laoghaire-Rathdown County Council continued throughout this period, but progress was very slow. A significant setback was experienced in February 2020 when the council was suddenly faced with the financial demands of managing Dún Laoghaire harbour.

In late 2020 the Friends took the initiative once again and, focusing on the upcoming centenary year of publication, set about campaigning with renewed vigour for local management. There was considerable assistance from local Minister of State Ossian Smyth TD, and the Department of Foreign Affairs. In a way, this underlined the place that James Joyce has assumed in Irish consciousness, a far cry from the early years of the Tower as described by Vivien Igoe. There were three sets of negotiations: Dún Laoghaire-Rathdown Council negotiated with the Office of

*A Personal History of the Joyce Tower and Museum*

Public Works for the lease on the Tower, and with Fáilte Ireland for care of the collection of artefacts. Having secured the lease and the collection, the council then concluded a licence agreement with a newly established management company, Joyce Tower and Museum CLG, a company limited by guarantee, which would be responsible for the day-to-day management of the Tower.

During the ten years of negotiation, the Friends had become increasingly proactive, organising and sponsoring programmes of activity in the Tower, particularly around Bloomsday, and on Joyce's birthday, 2 February. Strong collaborative links were established with other local cultural and heritage organisations such as dlrLexIcon, the Pavilion Theatre and Dalkey Castle and Heritage Centre. The annual celebrations spread out from the Tower: film shows and a painting exhibition in the dlrLexIcon; a unique performance of Geoffrey Molyneux Palmer's settings of *Chamber Music* in the Pavilion Theatre. A reading group on Joyce's work, led by Robert Walsh, was meeting regularly in Fitzgerald's pub in Sandycove. During the Covid pandemic, the group met online under Andrew Basquille's direction. Annual expeditions were organised to European locations associated with Joyce and with *Ulysses*: Paris, Trieste, Zurich, Szombathely … and Mullingar. On several occasions, the Friends hosted film crews from Ireland and abroad at the Tower. The value of the Friends of Joyce Tower to members during the Covid restrictions cannot be underestimated. During this time a succession of chairpersons led the organisation: Julia Beckett, James Holahan, the present author, and currently, Julie Larkin.

The museum project entered a new phase on 27 July 2022, when Joyce Tower and Museum CLG was licensed to manage the Tower on behalf of Dún Laoghaire-Rathdown County Council. The first board of the company comprised Frank Cogan (chairperson), Helen Gallivan, Trish Cronin, Séamus Cannon, Dave Lawless, Andrew Basquille and Deirdre Black. The board immediately prioritised the recruitment of a manager/curator and on 1 December 2022, Dr Alice Ryan, a Joycean scholar with experience of business management, took up the position. Alice's appointment heralds a new and exciting chapter in the history of the Tower as a unique Joyce Museum. It is a positive and optimistic note on which to conclude a history by previous curators Vivien Igoe and Robert Nicholson, who both made such valuable contributions.

*An Cathaoirleach of Dún Laoghaire-Rathdown County Council, Mary Hanafin, presents Frank Cogan, Chairperson of the board of Joyce Tower and Museum, with the key to the Tower, in a symbolic gesture to begin the new chapter in the life of the museum, September 2022*

# A BRIEF READING LIST

Bolton, Jason, Tim Carey, Rob Goodbody, and Gerry Clabby, *The Martello Towers of Dublin*, Dublin, Dún Laoghaire-Rathdown and Fingal County Council, 2012.

Bulfin, William, *Rambles in Eirinn*, Dublin, M.H. Gill & Son, 1907.

Colum, Padraic and Mary, *Our Friend James Joyce*, New York, Doubleday & Company, Inc., 1958.

Cronin, Anthony, *Dead as Doornails*, Dublin, The Dolmen Press, 1976.

Ellmann, Richard, *James Joyce's Tower*, Dublin, Eastern Regional Tourism Organisation Limited, Hely Thom, 1969.

——— *James Joyce (revised edition)*, New York, Oxford University Press, 1982.

Gogarty, Oliver St John, *It Isn't This Time of Year at All!*, London, Macgibbon and Kee, 1954.

Igoe, Vivien, *James Joyce's Dublin Houses & Nora Barnacle's Galway*, Dublin, The Lilliput Press, 2007.

——— *The Real People of Joyce's Ulysses: A Biographical Guide*, Dublin, University College Dublin Press, 2016.

Joyce, James, *Ulysses: The Corrected Text*, London, The Bodley Head/Penguin Books, 1986.

McCourt, John, *Consuming Joyce: 100 Years of Ulysses in Ireland*, London, Bloomsbury, 2022.

Nicholson, Robert, *The Ulysses Guide: Tours through Joyce's Dublin*, Dublin, New Island Books, 2019.

O'Connor, Ulick, *The Times I've seen: Oliver St. John Gogarty, A Biography*, New York, Ivan Obolensky, 1963.

O'Sullivan, Seumas, *Essays and Recollections*, Dublin, The Talbot Press, 1944.

Pearson, Peter and Frank Power, *The Forty Foot: A Monument to Sea Bathing*, Dublin, Environmental Publications, 1995.

Ryan, John, *Remembering How We Stood*, Dublin, The Lilliput Press, 2004.

Wall, Mervyn, *Forty Foot: Gentlemen Only*, Dublin, Allen Figgis, 1962.

# CURATOR BIOGRAPHIES

VIVIEN IGOE

Dr Vivien Igoe, a Dubliner, is a graduate of University College Dublin.

A former Curator of the Joyce Museum, she was involved with the organisation of the First and Second International James Joyce Symposia held in Dublin in 1967 and 1969. She was European Secretary of the International James Joyce Foundation; a founder member of the James Joyce Institute of Ireland; and was Chair of the Institute from 1980 to 1985.

Vivien worked as an editorial publicity officer with Bord Failte, the Irish Tourist Board, before moving to the Department of the Taoiseach as research consultant. She was heritage manager and archivist at the Royal Hospital, Kilmainham, and was responsible for the creation of the Pensioners' Museum and its collection of display items. Vivien is a founder member of the Francis Ledwidge Cottage Museum in Slane, Co. Meath. She is the author of five books and numerous articles, and has been a contributor to *Sunday Miscellany* on RTÉ Radio.

Her books include *James Joyce's Dublin Houses & Nora Barnacle's Galway* (The Lilliput Press, 2007); *A Literary Guide to*

*Dublin* (Methuen, 1994); *City of Dublin* (Pitkin, 1997); *Dublin Burial Grounds and Graveyards* (Wolfhound, 2001) and *The Real People of Joyce's Ulysses: A Biographical Guide* (UCD Press, 2016).

## ROBERT NICHOLSON

Robert Nicholson was born and lives in Dublin.

He graduated from Trinity College with a degree in English Language and Literature. For more than forty years he was Curator of the James Joyce Museum, retiring in 2019. He was also Curator of the Dublin Writers Museum from its foundation in 1991 and was responsible for establishing and displaying its collection.

He was secretary of the James Joyce Centenary committee and helped to organise the International James Joyce Symposia in Dublin in 1982 and 1992. He has been involved with the James Joyce Centre since its inception and is a member of its board of directors. He has been a member of the James Joyce Institute of Ireland since 1979 and was Chair from 1988 to 1992.

His book *The Ulysses Guide: Tours through Joyce's Dublin* was first published by Methuen in 1988 and he also wrote *The James Joyce Daybook* (Anna Livia Press, 1989). In 2007 he presented a DVD, *James Joyce's Dublin: The Ulysses Tour*, for Artsmagic. He has contributed articles and reviews to the *James Joyce Quarterly*, *The James Joyce Broadsheet*, *The James Joyce Centre Bloomsday Magazine* and numerous other publications.

In 2019 Dublin City Council presented Robert with the Senator David Norris Bloomsday Award for his lifetime contribution to Bloomsday and Joycean culture.

# ACKNOWLEDGEMENTS
# GO RAIBH MAITH AGAIBH

Apart from Vivien and Robert, many others contributed to *Tales from the Tower*.

Our thanks to all, but, in particular, to project advisers Dr Séamus Cannon and Andrew Basquille; to Breandán Ó Broin, our editor, and Carrie Fonseca, our editorial adviser.

Thanks are also due to the Martello Publishing team of Michael Darcy and Djinn von Noorden, and to editor Susan McKeever. Thanks also to literary agent Jonathan Williams for helping get the project started, artist Susan Early for the use of her work as cover illustration, and designer Niall McCormack for his work on layout and design.

# INDEX

1 Martello Terrace, Bray 25
2 Millbourne Avenue 36, 124
7 Eccles Street 5, 17, 55, 107, 131
    door knocker 31–3
15 Usher's Island 124–5
41 Brighton Square 45

*A Wake Newslitter* 15, 20, 22, 43, 54
Abbey Theatre 24, 51, 55, 90, 104
Abbott, Berenice 166
Acton, Charles 52
Aer Lingus 82
Ahern, Bertie 107
Anderson, Ernie 6
Anderson, Yvonne viii
Ando, Ichiro 62
Atherton, James 33
Aubert, Jacques 48
Auster, Paul 137

Balloonatics 99–100, 105, 107
Barkentin, Marjorie 33, 38
Barnacle (Joyce), Nora 79, 87, 89, 102, 132, 147, 160
Barry, Suzie viii
Basquille, Andrew 159, 164, 165, 173, 174
Bates, Denis xii, 69
BBC 41, 78, 81, 99, 125, 126, 141
Beach, Sylvia xi–xii, 6–7, 76, 124, 151
Beck, Harald 136
Beckett, Julia vii, 173
Beckett, Samuel 13, 38, 73, 76, 79, 83
Bekker, Pieter 84
Bell, G.K.A. 132
Bellow, Saul 63
Benstock, Bernard 39, 46, 48, 54, 61
Berkoff, Steven 94

Berryman, John 40
Bindervoet, Erik 148
Black, Deirdre 174
Blackshaw, Basil 12, 108
Bloomsday 3–4, 25–6, 47, 50, 55, 60, 62, 74, 77–9, 83, 87–8, 89, 92–3, 95, 98–100, 102–3, 104–5, 107, 116–19, 120–2, 131, 133, 138, 140, 144, 151–2, 156, 161, 164, 166, 173
    centenary 128, 129
    festival 96, 105
    Global 151
Bloomsday Pilgrimage 4
Boisen, Mogens 48
Bono 111
Bord Fáilte viii, 10, 40, 62–4, 118, 172 *see also* Fáilte Ireland
Bowen, Jack 48–9
Boyd Barrett, Richard 156–7, 158
Boyle, Bob 56
Brady, Paul 151
Braine, John 40–1
Brayden, William 104
Brown, Richard 84
Browne, Vincent vii–viii, 145, 171
Budgen, Mrs 43, 54
Budgen, Frank 43, 46, 48, 54
Buick, Robin 97
Bulfin, William 2, 132
Burgess, Anthony 81
Burke, Michael 14
Burton, Denis 117–18
Bute, Mary Ellen 37
Byrne, David 96, 104–5
Byrne, John Francis 17

Cameron, Catherine 3

# A Personal History of the Joyce Tower and Museum

Canal+ 125
Cannon, Séamus 161, 164, 166, 174
Cape Mortella, Corsica 1
Carey, Tim 137, 142–3
Carroll, Breda 121
Carroll, Jim 121
Carroll, Noel 26, 55, 61
Caviston, Peter 105
Ceannt, Éamonn 154
Channel 4 125, 162
Churchill, Sarah 52
Clancy, George 17
Clancy, Long John 162
Clery, Noelle 52
Clew, William J. 52
Cogan, Frank 174
Cole, Dorothy 5
Coleman, Aidan 164
Collinge, Lennie 74
Collins, Patrick 49, 78
Colum, Padraic 5, 8, 33, 44, 52
Comerford, Bernadette 143
Connolly, Colm 125
Connolly, Nora 99, 119
Copeland, Louis 135
Costello, Peter 43, 127
Crispi, Luca 128, 130
Croessmann, Harley K. 16
Croessmann Collection 16–17
Cronin, Anthony 4, 74
Cronin, Trish 174
Cummiskey, Roger 129
Curley, Marie 102
Curran, Constantine P. 3–4
Cusack, Cyril 8

Daalder, Tineke 35
Dalkey Castle 173
Dalkey Island 31
Dalton, Jack 56
Daly, Ciaran 96–7
Davey, Shaun 147
Davis, Gerald 119, 135
de Barra, Sadbh vii
de Fouw, Jan 102
Deane, John F. 125
Deane, Vincent 136
Delaney, Frank 79
Delimata, Bozena 23, 57, 60
Dempsey, George 101, 163
Devine, V.M. 163
Devlin, Barry 151

Devlin, Cormac 162, 164
Devlin, Martina 158
'Diceman' (Thom McGinty) 103, 107
Diddlem Club 117, 118
dlrLexIcon Library 59, 173
Dolan, Terry 100
Donnelly, Peter ('The Racker') 122, 132
Donohoe, John 129
Doyle, Danny 82
Doyle, Roddy 107
Dublin, UNESCO City of Literature 141
Dublin Joyce Society 3–5 *see also* Joyce Tower Society
Dublin Millennium 98
Dublin Theatre Festival (1969) 59
Dublin Tourism 105, 113–15, 130, 142
Dublin Tourism Enterprises 115
Dublin Writers Museum 59, 105–6, 108, 112, 113, 115–16, 129–30, 137–8, 142, 145, 153, 167
Duddy, Brendan 43, 50, 52
Dún Laoghaire Baths 13–14
Dún Laoghaire Borough Corporation 63
Dún Laoghaire-Rathdown County Council viii, ix, 142, 145, 154–5, 157, 160, 162, 167, 171–2, 174
Dunning, Brian 131
Dunphy, Eamon 133
Durcan, Paul 9

Eastern Regional Tourism 9, 43, 62–4, 70
Eblana Theatre 8
Eckley, Grace 87
Eco, Umberto 44, 47, 48
Eliot, T.S. 6
Ellis, Brian 101
Ellmann, Richard 26, 35, 42, 52, 55, 60, 79, 84, 97
Enright, Leo 126
European Academy of Poetry 125

Fáilte Ireland 142, 147, 152, 157, 160, 162, 167, 169, 171 *see also* Bord Fáilte
Farrell, Gerry 89, 99
Farrell, James T. 66
Farrington, Colin 107
Feeley, John 141, 143, 148, 150, 161
Ferguson, Ruth 144, 154
Feshbach, Sidney 46
Field, Saul 51
Fitzgerald, Mike viii
Fitzgerald, Tom vii, 105, 171
Fitzpatrick Travel Films 30–1

Flynn, Pat vii
Forkner, Ben 41
Forty Foot Bathing Place 1, 11, 118, 120, 125, 126
Frank, Nino 76
Freund, Gisèle 76
Freyer, Grattan 52
Friedan, Betty 94
Friends of Joyce Tower vii–viii, ix–x, xiii, 145–6, 148, 152–3, 156, 160, 165, 171–3
*see also* James Joyce Tower and Museum

Gallagher, Darina 159–60, 166
Gallivan, Helen 174
*Gamble No Gamble* 24
Garvin, John 3, 7, 8, 25–6, 50, 52, 59, 60
Gaynor, Peter 152
Gébler Davies, Stan 104
Geldof, Bob 95
Gell-Mann, Murray 126
'Geragh', Sandycove xi, 3, 61–3
Giedion-Welcker, Carola 12, 89–90
Gilbert, Stuart 6
Gleeson, Kay vii
Glynn, Patrick vii
Gogan, Robert 158
Gogarty, Oliver D. 7, 35–6
Gogarty, Oliver St John xi, 2–3, 7, 36, 97, 101, 110, 130, 132, 167
Goodbody, Nora xii, 14, 69
Goodbody, Rob vii
Goodbody, Wendy 161, 164, 166
Gordon, John 136
Gordimer, Nadine 99
Gorman, Herbert 6
Gorman, Michael 39–40, 43
Gotham Book Mart 7, 9, 24–5, 37
Grafton Singers 158
Greene, Roger 97
Griffith, Arthur 2
Groden, Michael 126
Guinness, Mrs Desmond 55
Gunn, Ian 136
Gunning, Des 96, 121

Hackett, Felix 43
Haines, Fred 25
Halper, Nathan 38
Hamilton, Richard 115, 127
Haran, Tom 129
Harford, Val 24
Harmon, Maurice 43

Harrington, Judith 136
Hart, Clive 15, 20, 30–2, 39, 48, 51, 52, 84, 100, 136
Hartnett, Michael 9
Hastings, Máire 9
Havel, Václav 118
Healy, Shay 82
Heaney, Catherine 151
Heaney, Marie 151
Heaney, Seamus 94, 99, 151
Hebald, Milton 26, 46, 49
Hedberg, Johannes 35
Hedlund, Magnus 35
Heffernan, Honor 158
Henchy, Patrick 37–8
Henkes, Robbert-Jan 148
Herbert, Stacey 129
Heritage Council 134–5
Herron, Colm 138
Hickey, Kieran 81
Higel, Edwin 97
Higgins, Michael D. 94, 125
Higgins, Sabina 152
Hodgart, Matthew 56
Holahan, James 158, 174
Holloway, Nuala 119
Horia, Vintilă 57
Horstmann, Fritzi 129
Huberman, Mark 128
Hulgraine, Charlie vii
Huston, John xii, 5, 6, 45, 125
Hustvedt, Siri 137
Hutchins, Patricia 127
Hutton, Patricia 85

Igoe, Vivien ix, xii, 70, 76, 87, 104, 107, 127, 128, 136, 141, 145, 162, 172
Imre, Szemethy 56–7
Inglis, Tony 116
Ireland, John de Courcy 52
Irish Georgian Society 55
Italian Cultural Centre 85
Italian National Television 31

James Joyce Centre 59, 83, 93, 96, 117, 134, 151
James Joyce Foundation (International) 30, 48, 54, 61
James Joyce Institute of Ireland 70, 120, 132, 166
*James Joyce Quarterly* 15, 30, 39, 40, 42, 54, 60, 72, 130

# A Personal History of the Joyce Tower and Museum

James Joyce societies
  Canada 17
  New York 7, 37
  Sweden and Finland 159
James Joyce Summer School, Dublin 100
James Joyce Symposium, International 93, 112, 131, 144
  First (1967) 39–40, 42–8
  Second (1969) 53–6
  1977: 70
  1980: 76
  Centenary (1982): 83–4
James Joyce Tower and Museum *see also* Friends of Joyce Tower
  closure xii, 62–3, 145
  construction xi, 1
  damp 53–4, 61–3, 92, 123, 158
  display cases 75
  exhibition space 12
  exhibitions 24, 58–9, 112, 131
  extension 71–2, 91, 154
  flagpole 124
  gunpowder magazine 12–13, 71, 74, 86, 90, 91, 92, 111, 125
  inventories 110, 115, 134, 149, 155, 162–3
  Joyce Centre, planned 60–3
  layout 70, 73–4
  library 15–16, 49, 91–2, 119, 162
  museum, plans for 3, 5
  opening: 6–8; fiftieth anniversary 144
  ownership xiii, 1–3, 10, 142–3, 149, 157, 167–9, 171–4
  pigeons 133, 139
  reduced hours 137, 143–4
  refurbishments 109, 123–4, 148, 153–5, 157–8
  register 106, 108, 114–15, 119, 155, 163, 165–7
  reopening 74
  reorganisation 110–11
  repairs 61
  restoration 64–5
  round room 107–10, 154, 158
  slideshows 79, 86
  souvenirs 91
  valuation 162
  visitors 18–19, 23, 39, 49, 94
  volunteers viii, xii, 145–7, 152–3, 157–8, 169, 171
  water supply 158
Johnston, Denis 6, 7, 75
Jolas, Eugene 7
Jolas, Maria 6, 7, 76

Joyce, Asta 43, 47
Joyce, Bob 93, 140
Joyce, Carol 159
Joyce, Giorgio 21, 43–4, 46–8
Joyce, James
  birthday 103, 153, 158, 173
  cabin trunk 85, 111
  centenary 75–6, 81–5, 93
  collections 64, 84
  commemorative coin 148
  courses on 51–2
  death mask 12, 44, 82, 89–90, 92, 111, 125
  documentaries on 50–1, 77, 98, 128–9
  estate 112, 130, 139–40, 141
  exhibitions 55 *see also* James Joyce Tower and Museum
  guitar 21, 23, 58, 111, 141, 143–4, 148, 150
  letters 55, 111
  memorabilia 21, 36, 101, 116, 129, 160
  notebooks 126
  piano 57–9, 72–3, 108
  plaques 97–8, 130
  portraits 12, 50, 82, 108, 166
  ration book 129
  recordings 92, 118
  spectacles 149–50
  statues 26, 49
  stays at the Tower 2–3
  tie 73, 111
  waistcoat 12–13, 34, 111
  wallet 49
  works:
  'The Cat and the Devil' 75
  *Chamber Music* 100, 135
  copyright 130, 139, 142
  'Day of the Rabblement' 102
  'The Dead' 124
  drafts 126
  *Dubliners* 44, 134, 156
  *Exiles* 95
  *Finnegans Wake*: 32, 69–70, 75, 87, 126, 159; film 37; tour 44
  first editions 77, 95, 134, 135, 160
  music in 56
  *Our Exagmination* 160
  *Portrait of the Artist as a Young Man* 17, 25, 36, 95, 101
  translations 35, 54, 62, 92, 99, 119
  *Ulysses*: vii, xi, 6–7, 56, 83, 88, 164; 'Aeolus' 22; 'Circe' 121; 'Cranly' 17; 'Cyclops' 117; film 25, 27–9, 36, 59, 125, 127; first editions 77, 129; illustrations 89; 'Ithaca' 157; 'Lestrygonians' 98, 102, 159; map

7, 87, 97; 'Nausicaa' 116; 'Penelope' 112; places in 34; plaques 97–8; play 33; recording (RTÉ) 83; 'Telemachus' 12, 50, 52, 117, 120, 126, 152, 166; 'Throwaway' 88–9; 'Wandering Rocks' 83
*Work in Progress* 83, 92, 116, 163–4
Joyce, Joe 104
Joyce, Lucia 77, 81, 160
Joyce, Nelly 57–8, 73
Joyce, Nora *see* Barnacle, Nora
Joyce, Stanislaus 45, 73, 101, 129, 132
Joyce, Stephen 76, 90–1, 98, 100, 102, 112, 130–1, 139
Joyce, Tom 4
Joyce Tower Society (Dublin Joyce Society) 8–9, 87, 125, 129, 163
Joyce Week (1962) 8

Kain, Richard 6, 8, 17–18, 48
Kavanagh, Patrick 4, 23–4
Keating, Thomas J. xii, 64, 66
Keegan, Owen 142–3, 157
Kelly, Frank 151
Kelly, Seamus ('Quidnunc') 3, 5–6, 12, 26, 46–7, 59, 60
Kenner, Hugh 84
Kenny, Pat 152, 158
Kiberd, Declan 75, 145
Kidd, John 112–13
Kiely, Benedict 41, 66
Killeen, Terence 144, 145, 148
Kilty, Brendan 124–5
Kinsella, Thomas 125
Knuth, Leo 50, 52

Lange, David 94
Language Centre of Ireland 52
Lantern Theatre 36
Larbaud, Valéry 99
Larkin, Julie 173
Lavin, Mary 7
Lawless, Dave 174
le Brocquy, Louis 82
*LÉ James Joyce* 159
Lee, Gerard 52
Leinwall, George 48, 61, 64
Léon, Alex 76, 112
Léon, Paul 112, 126
*Lettres Nouvelles* 19
Leventhal, A.J. 4, 6, 8
Leventhal, Con 163
Levin, Harry 51

Lewinski, Jorge 80
Lidderdale, Jane 58, 76–7, 82
Liddy, James 8
Linehan, Rosaleen 125
Lines, Graham 27
Liss, Joseph 48
Looby, John 45
Lucchesi, Alvaro 128
Lyons, J.B. 43, 60

Mac Anna, Tomás 51
McCarthy, Fergal 141
MacCarvill, Eileen 8, 23, 26, 43, 49, 50, 52, 60
McConnell, A.J. 55
McCourt, John 81, 128
MacDonagh, Donagh 5, 7, 26, 36
MacDonagh, Niall 8–9
McGinty, Thom ('The Diceman') 103, 107
McGovern, Barry 102–3, 105, 117, 121–3, 131, 139–40, 144–5, 152, 159
McGregor, Ewan 118
McHugh, Roger 26, 43, 46, 49, 50
McHugh, Roland xii, 33, 69–70, 104
McKenna, T.P. 24, 27, 49
McLelland, Alan, *Bloomsday* 8
McManus, Áine 15, 30
McManus, Don viii
MacNeice, Louis 7
McSharry, Katherine 128
Mc Sweeney, Brenda 145
Maddox, Brenda 102
Mahony, Michael 163
*Marques* 78
Martello Tower, Sandycove *see* James Joyce Tower and Museum
Martello towers 1
Martin, Augustine 52, 100
Martin, Patrick 129
Mathews, P.J. 128
Mellows, Elgin W. 55
Miles, Sarah 94
Milesian flag 6–7, 50
Minghella, Edana 159
Minstrel Tours (CIE) 38–9
Minujín, Marta 78
Moloney, Mary Pat 159, 161–2
Monaghan, Kevin 60, 93, 107, 127
Monaghan, May 7, 25, 34, 37–8
Montgomery, Niall 3, 6, 8, 43, 50, 54, 60
Morrissey, Eamon 9, 75, 77, 129, 164
Morrison, George 96
Morrow, Antoinette 139, 140

# A Personal History of the Joyce Tower and Museum

Moseley, Virginia 30
Muglins, the 31
Muldoon, Paul 151
Muldoon's Picnic 133
Mullen, Philip 99
Murayama, Eitaro 33–4
Murphy, Catherine 139
Murphy, Pat 118
Murphy, Sinéad 166
Murphy, Tom 15, 50
Murray, Bryan 159, 164, 166
Museum of Literature Ireland (MoLI) 30, 154
Museum Standards Programme for Ireland (MSPI) 134–5, 138
Myers, Jack 104
Myers, Kevin 104

na gCopaleen, Myles (Brian O'Nolan) 3–4
Nash, David 78
National Defence Act (1804) 1
National Library of Ireland 126, 130, 154
Naylor, Harold 9–10, 22–3, 47
Nelson's Pillar, O'Connell Street 22
Ní Threasaigh, Caitríona 156, 159, 161–2, 164
Nicholson, Robert vii, ix, xii, 172, 174
Norman, H.F. 155–6
Norris, David 7–8, 70, 75, 76, 93, 113, 127, 132, 133, 158
Nutting, Maurice 129

O'Connor, Joseph 145
O'Connor, Ulick 26, 52, 75
O'Conor, Hugh 127–8
O'Doherty, Eamon 89, 102
O'Driscoll, Bob 77–8
O'Driscoll, Treasa 77–8
O'Faoláin, Seán 6, 7
O'Flaherty, Gerard (Gerry) 16, 26, 43–4, 46, 48, 50, 52, 54, 60–1, 128, 136, 144
O'Grady, Noel 166
O'Hanlon, Ardal 162
O'Hanlon, John 88
O'Hanrahan, Paul 100, 105, 118, 126, 142
O'Kelly, Michael 86, 96
Okri, Ben 159
O'Mahony, Eoin 52
O'Meara, David 156
Ó Mórdha, Seán 77, 97, 128
O'Neill, Christine and Tim 167
O'Nolan, Brian (Myles na gCopaleen) 3–4
Ó Nualláin, Micheál 78
Order of the Finnegans 140, 161
O'Regan, Maebh 152

O'Regan, Seán 152
O'Rourke, Fran 141, 143, 148, 150, 161
Orpen, Bea 60
Orwell, Sonia 53
Osawa, Kayoshi 62
Osawa (O'Sawa), Masayoshi 62
O'Shea, Milo 59
Osman, John 104
O'Sullivan, Ciara 24
O'Sullivan, Seán 12
O'Sullivan, Tomás 8
O'Toole, Dermot 22–3

Palmer, Geoffrey Molyneux 100, 173
Parker, Virginia 150
Paulin, Tom 125
Pavilion Theatre 173
Peacock Theatre 55, 77
Pearl, Cyril 33
PEN conference (1971) 62
Plant, Derrick 48
Pollock, Harry 17, 55
Potts, Willard 84
Power, Arthur 51, 59
Pritchett, V. S. 19
Probst, Graham 27
Prunty, Malachy 160

Quidnunc *see* Kelly, Seamus

'Racker' (Peter Donnelly) 122, 132
Reid, Alec 79
Reilly, Tom 134
Reynolds, Lorna 43
Robbins, Paddy 65
Robinson, Dolly 8
Robinson, Lennox 3
Robinson, Tina 96, 121
Rodgers, W.R. 7
Roe, Owen 161–2
Roeves, Maurice 27, 29–30
Rogers, W.G. 25
ROSC International Art Exhibition (1980) 78
Rose, Danis 88
Rose, David 119
Roth, Samuel 82
RTÉ 18, 60, 77, 83, 99, 118, 125, 128, 140, 143, 145, 161
Ruggiero, Bertha 21
Ruggiero, Paul 20–2
Rushdie, Salman 114
Rushe, Desmond 21–2, 64
Ruskin, John 82

Russel, Myra 84, 100
Ryan, Alice x, xiii, 174
Ryan, John 4–5, 24, 74, 78, 86, 95, 129, 165
Ryan, Patricia 24

Sandycove xi, 1, 11, 71, 133, 141, 158, 163, 173
Schaurek, Eileen 7, 23
Schiff, Dan 92, 102
Schmitz, Ettore (Italo Svevo) 59
Schoonbroodt, Jean 48
Schorman, Walter 90
Schuller, Charles 24
Scott, Michael xi–xii, 3, 5, 7, 18, 60–1, 63, 71, 86, 90, 95
Scott, Niall 71
Scott Tallon Walker Architects 71
Scudds, Anna viii
Scudds, Colin viii
Seager, Pat 108
Seiden, Fredric 32–3
Seigne, Phyllis 162
Semmler, Clem 33
Senn, Fritz 15–16, 20–2, 36–7, 39–40, 48, 50, 54, 61, 84, 113, 128, 136
Shakespeare and Company xi, 6, 164
Sheehy Skeffington, Andrée 102
Sheehy Skeffington, Francis 102
Sheridan, Monica 50
Sheridan, Niall 6
Simpson, John 136
Skeffington, F.J.C. (Francis Sheehy Skeffington) 102
Slomczynski, Maciej 54
Slote, Sam 130, 136
Slovak, Charlotte 128–9
Smyth, Ossian 172
Solomon, Margaret 46
Soupault, Philippe 76
Southwell, Gary 143
Speck, Paul 12, 89–90
Staley, Tom 15, 39, 46, 47, 48, 54, 55
Starkey, James 132
Stead, Alistair 84
Stead, W.T. 87
Steloff, Frances 6, 7, 24–5, 37, 51
Stephens, Davy 104
Steyn, Stella 116
Straumann, Heinrich 51
Strick, Joseph 25–7, 38, 59, 125
Sullivan, John 160

Sullivan, Kevin 37
Suttle, Sam 5
Sweeney, Eric 161
Svevo, Italo (Ettore Schmitz) 59
Svevo, Letizia 81

Takács, Ferenc 159
Take 5 Theatre Company 105
Taylor, Ciaran 106, 113, 115
Taylor Black, Donald 97
Theroux, Alexander Louis 34
Tidy Towns Association 145
Tindall, William York 37–8
Trench, Chalmers (Terry) 60
Trench, Dermot (Richard Samuel) Chenevix xi, 2–3, 36, 60
Trilling, Lionel 37
Tubridy, Ryan 118
TV3 133

UCD, Aula Maxima 153–4
*Ulysses Guide* 97–8, 127, 136, 139, 159
UNESCO cities of literature 141, 161
Urnov, Mikael 33

Varadkar, Leo viii, 156, 160
Veale, Eileen 10, 25–6, 38, 43, 50, 60
Veale, Tom 48
Vila-Matas, Enrique 140
Vilar, Sergio 19

Walcott, Derek 99
Wall, Mervyn 26, 50
Walsh, Robert 173
Walsh, Seán 127–8
Ward, Andrew 166
Ward, David 30, 47, 48, 61
Warner, Francis 46, 48
Weaver, Harriet 77
Wilder, Thornton 6
Worthington, Mabel 56

Yared, Aida 136
Yeats, John Butler 155
Youell, Adrian 50
Youell, Siew 50
Youell, Vivi 50

Zurich 20–1, 26
Zurich James Joyce Foundation 20, 136